# Data and Decision Sciences - Recent Advances and Applications

*Edited by Tien M. Nguyen*

Published in London, United Kingdom

Data and Decision Sciences - Recent Advances and Applications
http://dx.doi.org/10.5772/intechopen.100865
Edited by Tien M. Nguyen

Contributors
Harun Sümbül, Marc Juanpera, Laia Ferrer-Martí, Marianna Garfí, Bruno Domenech, Rafael Pastor, Chioma Ngozi Nwafor, Bernard Cadet, Isabel Cuadrado Gordillo, Andrzej Łodziński, Tien M. Nguyen



First published in London, United Kingdom, 2023 by IntechOpen
IntechOpen is the global imprint of INTECHOPEN LIMITED, registered in England and Wales, registration number: 11086078, 5 Princes Gate Court, London, SW7 2QJ, United Kingdom
Printed in Croatia

British Library Cataloguing-in-Publication Data
A catalogue record for this book is available from the British Library

Additional hard and PDF copies can be obtained from orders@intechopen.com

Data and Decision Sciences - Recent Advances and Applications
Edited by Tien M. Nguyen
p. cm.

This title is part of the Business, Management and Economics Book Series, Volume 9
Topic: Business and Management
Series Editor: Taufiq Choudhry
Topic Editor: Vito Bobek and Tatjana Horvat

Print ISBN 978-1-80356-287-2
Online ISBN 978-1-80356-288-9
eBook (PDF) ISBN 978-1-80356-289-6
ISSN 2753-894X

For EU product safety concerns:
IN TECH d.o.o., Prolaz Marije Krucifikse Kozulić 3, 51000 Rijeka, Croatia,
info@intechopen.com or visit our website at intechopen.com.

IntechOpen Book Series

# Business, Management and Economics

Volume 9

## Aims and Scope of the Series

This series will provide a comprehensive overview of recent research trends in business and management, economics, and marketing. Topics will include asset liability management, financial consequences of the financial crisis and covid-19, financial accounting, mergers and acquisitions, management accounting, SMEs, financial markets, corporate finance and governance, managerial technology and innovation, resource management and sustainable development, social entrepreneurship, corporate responsibility, ethics and accountability, microeconomics, labour economics, macroeconomics, public economics, financial economics, econometrics, direct marketing, creative marketing, internet marketing, market planning and forecasting, brand management, market segmentation and targeting and other topics under business and management. This book series will focus on various aspects of business and management whose in-depth understanding is critical for business and company management to function effectively during this uncertain time of financial crisis, Covid-19 pandemic, and military activity in Europe.

# Meet the Series Editor

Prof. Choudhry holds a BSc degree in Economics from the University of Iowa, as well as a Masters and Ph.D. in Applied Economics from Clemson University, USA. In January 2006, he became a Professor of Finance at the University of Southampton Business School. He was previously a Professor of Finance at the University of Bradford Management School. He has over 80 articles published in international finance and economics journals. His research interests and specialties include financial econometrics, financial economics, international economics and finance, housing markets, financial markets, among others.

# Meet the Volume Editor

Dr. Tien Nguyen serves as an adjunct research professor in Mathematics at California State University, Fullerton (CSUF), where he is also a visiting scholar and chairman of the advisory board of the Center of Computational and Applied Mathematics. He also serves as a senior project leader at The Aerospace Corporation, California. Prior to this position, Dr. Nguyen was an associate director, interim director, and principal engineer/technical staff. He is a retired engineering fellow and chief engineer at Raytheon. Previously, he worked at the NASA Jet Propulsion Laboratory and served as NASA delegate to the International Consultative Committee for Space Data System (CCSDS). Dr. Nguyen received his Ph.D. in Applied Mathematics from Claremont Graduate University, California. He holds 16 patents with three pending. His current research interests include the application of data analytics, decision sciences, and support systems for space applications.

# Contents

# Preface

The current rapid development of data science, involving data mining, predictive analytics, statistics, Artificial Intelligence (AI), and machine learning, has been extended to decision science supporting decision-making processes in the presence of uncertainty. A great deal of work has been accomplished by many authors on the topics associated with data science and decision science, but a reference book on the combined Data and Decision Sciences (DDS) is rare. This book is intended to serve as a professional technical book that presents a collection of chapters addressing recent advances and applications of the combined DDS. The book is planned to provide a source of reference for educators, engineers, scientists, and researchers in the fields of DDS. The objective of this book is to compile a set of chapters with associated topics capturing recent advancements of DDS across a wide range of applications that are common to the combined data and decision sciences. To achieve this objective, the book is organized into four sections with topics related to (i) recent advances and application of combined DDS in future space-based applications, business, medical, and agriculture, optimization modeling in decision science, and (ii) new perspective on the cognitive decision-making process. This book is organized as follows:

Section 1 – "Overview of DDS and Recent Advancement in Future Space Application"

This section includes two chapters, including Chapter 1 and Chapter 2. Chapter 1 is an introductory chapter that provides an overview of DDS and discusses the differences between data science and decision science. Chapter 2 describes a DDS application for a future space system addressing a combined DDS technology using machine learning and artificial intelligence (ML-AI) for a ground-based high-power amplifier pre-distorter operated in an unknown operating environment.

Section 2 – "Recent DDS Advancements in Business, Medical, and Agriculture Applications"

This section compiles three chapters, namely, Chapters 3, 4 and 5 with emphasis on the combined DDS applications in business, medical, and agriculture fields. Chapter 3 discusses a combined DDS approach using Monte Carlo simulation methods to generate desired data for making strategic business decisions. Chapter 4 presents another combined DDS approach for medical applications using ML-AI and regression analysis along with the Ordinary Least Squares (OLS) method for predicting lung vital capacity. Finally, Chapter 5 proposes an innovative decision approach using an integrated multicriteria decision-making process in the presence of uncertainty. The proposed approach is applied to a specific use case for the selection of the most sustainable technology to improve a small-scale farm in Colombia.

Section 3 – "Optimization Modeling in Decision Science"

This section includes Chapter 6. Chapter 6 proposes a mathematical model of a decision support system using a multi-criteria optimization approach. The proposed model is demonstrated for solving the bicriteria problem.

Section 4 – "A New Perspective on Cognitive Decision-Making Process"

This section consists of Chapter 7 with an emphasis on cognitive decision-making in dynamic systems. This chapter discusses the cognitive decision systems involved with the intervention of complex, dynamic and changeable systems that can generate imprecisions, difficulties, or even incorrect decisions.

I would like to recognize the contributions of several key people to the creation of this professional technical book and express my deep gratitude to all the authors and coauthors for their contributions and several anonymous reviewers. The success of this book has not only been the result of the work of the authors, coauthors, and reviewers but also from the cooperation of several people at the IntechOpen publisher who provided constant support. Particularly, I would like to thank (i) the IntechOpen Publishing Process Managers, Ms. Jelena Vrdoljak, Ms. Patricia Kerep, and Ms. Karmen Đaleta for their invaluable assistance, conscientious, and relentless support during the review process, editing and publishing process - without them, this book is not possible; (ii) Commissioning Editor, Ms. Jelena Germuth, for her constant support; (iii) my colleagues from Carolina State University and California State University in Fullerton for their continuous support and review of a couple of chapters of this book; and (iv) my manager at The Aerospace Corporation, Dr. Tony Tang, for his constant support. Finally, I'm forever indebted to my wonderful wife, Thu-Hang Nguyen, for her patience, encouragement, and continuous support during the process of making this professional technical book.

**Tien M. Nguyen**
Adjunct Research Professor,
Chair of the CCAM Advisory Board,
Center for Computational and Applied Mathematics (CCAM),
California State University in Fullerton (CSUF),
Fullerton, California, USA

The Aerospace Corporation,
USA

Section 1

# Overview of DDS and Recent Advancement in Future Space Application

**Chapter 1**

# Introductory Chapter: Overview of Data and Decision Sciences – Recent Advances and Applications

*Tien M. Nguyen*

## 1. Introduction

Due to the rapid growth of big data analytics related to all aspects of human activities, the surge in decision-making complexity due to the current climate of uncertainty with unforeseen consequences, and the increasing pervasiveness of advanced information and communication technologies (ICT) such as the proliferation of mobile applications, Internet-of-Things, and bots, we have witnessed an acceleration of integration of many complex ICT systems-of-systems (SoS) and social networks across of a wide spectrum of application domains that include, but are not limited to, telecommunications, satellite communications, medicine, military, education, agriculture, arts, and culture. The primary motivation for this book is to compile some of the latest research work addressing recent advances and applications of data and decision sciences (DDS) across the above-mentioned application domains. This book is a collective effort that uses a diverse set of studies and investigations to cover a wide spectrum of DDS applications. The goal is to shed some insights into the use of DDS models for assisting data analysts and decision-makers.

The objective of this introductory chapter is two-fold, namely, to provide (i) an overview of the data science and decision science, (ii) recent advances and DSS applications with an emphasis on machine learning and artificial intelligence (ML-AI), and (iii) overview and understanding of recent DDS applications. The remaining of this chapter is organized as follows:

- Section 2 provides an overview of data science and decision science.
- Section 3 discusses the differences between data science and decision science and recent advances in DDS.
- Section 4 concludes the chapter with final remarks on the DDS trends.

## 2. Overview data science, and decision science

### 2.1 Data science

Data science is a relatively new and emerging field of research for many mathematicians, statisticians, scientists, and engineers in the world. It has been derived from data mining along with statistical analysis. It is defined in Cambridge Dictionary as "the use of scientific methods to obtain useful information from computer data, especially large amounts of data [1]". In a more technical detail definition in Dictionary.com, it is defined as a field that "deals with advanced data analytics and modeling, using mathematics, statistics, programming, and machine learning to extract valuable, often predictive information from large data sets [2]". Practically, IBM defines data science as a science field, which combines mathematics and statistics, specialized programming languages, advanced data analytics, artificial intelligence (AI), and machine learning (ML) with specific subject matter expertise to uncover actionable insights hidden in an organization's data. These insights can be used to guide decision-making and strategic planning [3]. A data science life cycle used by the industry is captured on the home page of the University of California in Berkley, School of Information [4]. The data science life cycle includes five stages, namely, (i) Stage 1 – data capture stage: data acquisition, data entry, signal reception, and data extraction; (ii) Stage 2 – data maintenance stage: data warehousing, data cleansing, data staging, data processing, data architecture; (iii) Stage 3: data mining processing stage: data mining, clustering/classification, data modeling, data summarization; (iv) Stage 4 – data analysis stage: exploratory/confirmatory, predictive analysis, regression, text mining, qualitative analysis; and (v) Stage 5 – communication stage: data reporting, data visualization, business intelligence, decision making. In the context of this book, this Subsection 2.1 focuses on IBM's definition and data processing and analysis stages of the data science life cycle, including data mining, machine learning and artificial intelligence (ML-AI) using neural networks and deep learning, statistical learning, and Bayesian statistics.

#### *2.1.1 Data mining*

Big data analytics (BDA) is defined as the process of exploiting and extracting meaningful information from a large and complex collection of data[1]. Data mining is one of the key required functions in the BDA process. It's well-known that the BDA process is part of the data science[1] life cycle, including five data processing stages. As pointed out earlier, the data processing Stage 3 is the data mining processing (DMP) to discover data patterns from a large collection of data [5–8]. **Figure 1** illustrates the DMP characteristics, including the types of data that can be mined and analyzed, the kinds of data mining patterns, data mining techniques, and applications.

As shown in **Figure 1**, DMP can be performed on various types of data such as (i) data from databases collected past and current banking data or experimental data from a complex satellite system; (ii) data from data warehouses, e.g., Amazon data warehouse contained mass data from Amazon business transactions collected from multiple sources and stored in a unified schema; (iii) actual daily real-time transaction data from the banks, e.g., credit approvals, check approvals, payment approvals, etc.; and (iv) other type of data includes but not limited to data collected from information technology (IT) system, data collected from health care and medical sciences, data collected from military defense systems such as images, video data streams, etc. For the kinds of data mining patterns, one of the key components of the data mining patterns is the characterization and discrimination of the features of a target class of data objects against the other features of objects from one or multiple contrasting target classes. After characterization and discrimination processing, the

[1] https://www.bmc.com/blogs/big-data-vs-analytics/.

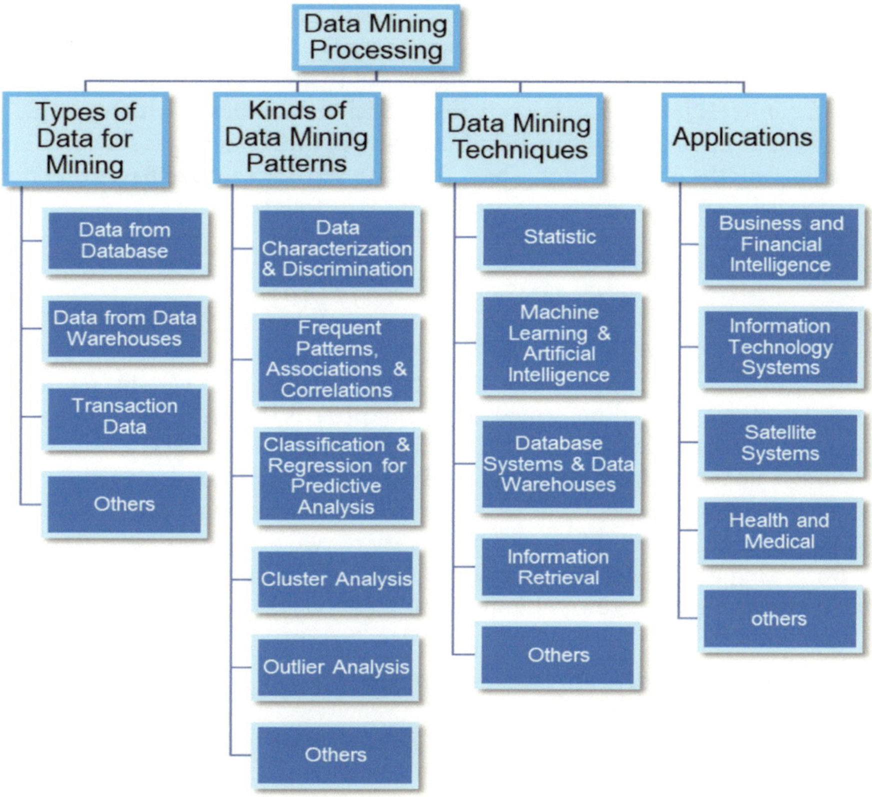


**Figure 1.**
*Data mining processing (DMP) characteristics.*

data is analyzed for frequent patterns using association and statistical correlation analyses. An example of the frequent pattern analysis is to study the behavior of the computer consumers in terms of how often and the types of the computer they buy, the software they buy, and the buyers' profession and their income ranges.

Within the context of this chapter, the following subsections will discuss ML-AI and statistical methods of interest to the data mining techniques as shown in **Figure 1**.

### *2.1.2 ML-AI, statistical learning, and Bayesian statistics*

ML-AI techniques are usually used for estimating and predicting the data characteristics and associated data trends. For examples, ML-AI can be used to analyze big data to predict stock market trends [9], and analysis of big consumer data can help the suppliers to forecast trends of customer behavior, markets, prices, and so on [10]. When the data content has several categorical variables, the prediction can be achieved through classification and pattern recognition. As an example, ML-AI using supervised learning and support vector machine (SVM) can be used to (i) predict the impacts of signal distortions caused by non-ideal satellite operational environment to the transmitted signal components, and (ii) classify the source of signal distortions [11]. In terms of ML-AI, past data is used to train the system, thus the newly accumulated data represents the case of repeat "modeling" where new data will be used to predict the trend in the future or classify an object (e.g., signal component) to a group (e.g., source of signal distortion) by comparing with the old data. Majority of practical and useful ML-AI modeling techniques are usually stochastic or statical in nature. Therefore, the term statistical learning is also used in literature for ML-AI modeling. As pointed out in [12], Bayesian is a way of practicing statistics in which the ML-AI modeling is built upon probability distributions, i.e., the modeling is solely calibrating and adjusting the probabilities. Thus, Bayesian statistics utilize Bayes theorem and facilitate the calculation of posterior distributions as follows:

$$p(\theta / data) \propto p(data / \theta)\, x\, p(\theta) \qquad (1)$$

Where $p(\theta / data)$ is the posterior probability distribution, $p(data / \theta)$ is the likely hood or the classification probability, and $p(\theta)$ is the prior probability.

Bayesian functional data analytical techniques include multiple curve-fitting (MCF), single neuronal analysis (SNA), and population-level analysis (PLA) [12]. MCF uses hierarchical modeling of firing intensity curves using BARS (i.e., BAR chart) approach. SNA is used for testing equality of two or more curves. Finally, PLA is used for testing equality of two groups of curves. As examples, MCF, SNA, and PLA have been used in health care and biology applications [13–15], respectively.

### *2.1.3 ML-AI using neural network and deep learning*

ML-AI modeling uses neural networks (NN) and deep learning (DL) to model the neuronal cells and their intricate functionality, and networking for processing the data (i.e., information) [12]. The terminology NN-DL or deep NN (DNN) is usually used to indicate a network that has more than two hidden layers with an input layer and one output layer with multiple nodes, as shown in **Figure 2** [12, 16]. The variables $x_i, w_i^{(m)}$, and $y_j$ are the DNN's parameters that are defined as the input node, weight of the hidden layer node, and the output node, respectively. As pointed out in [16] DNN model has more hidden layers, which requires longer simulation time and more training data storage.

The DNN modeling requires (i) characterizing the DNN's system parameters and the associated "loss" function in terms of the weight parameter $w_i^{(m)}$, and (ii) tune these parameters using the training data collected by the system architect under controlled environment. **Figure 3** provides a high-level description of the key DNN tuning parameters, including layer size and related mini-batch size for numerical approximation of gradient, gradient threshold, and learning rate. **Figure 3(a)** illustrates the layer size; **Figure 3(b)** shows the exploding gradient if the "terms" in the differential equation are greater than 1, and **Figure 3(c)** depicts the learning rate. **Figure 3(c)** shows that the learning rate can have a large learning rate and a small learning rate that can be used for fast adaptation during data acquisition phase and slow adaptation during tracking phase after the loss function is converged. Note that a differential equation is usually used to characterize a neural network layer.

In practice for DNN, there are usually four hyper-parameters to tune, namely, layer size, mini-batch size, gradient threshold, and learning rate. Tuning the layer size to select the best size to produce the best manageable agent size of training data meaning that the layer size should be selected to optimize the required training

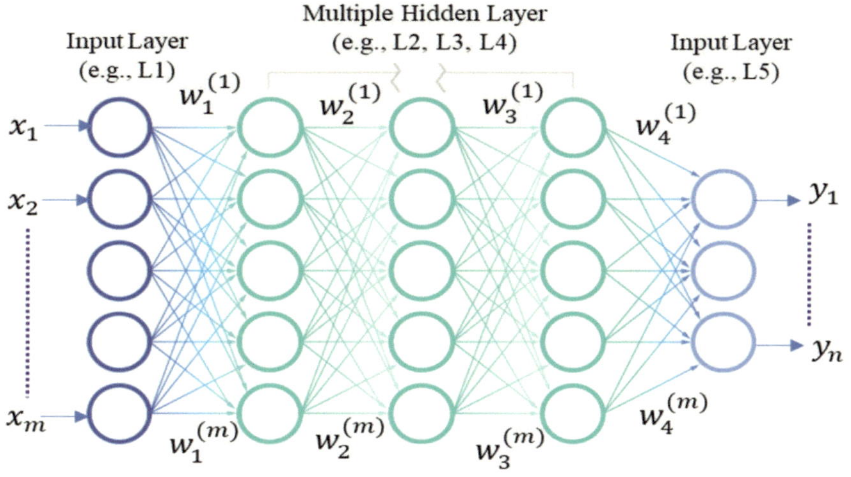


**Figure 2.**
*Deep neural network.*

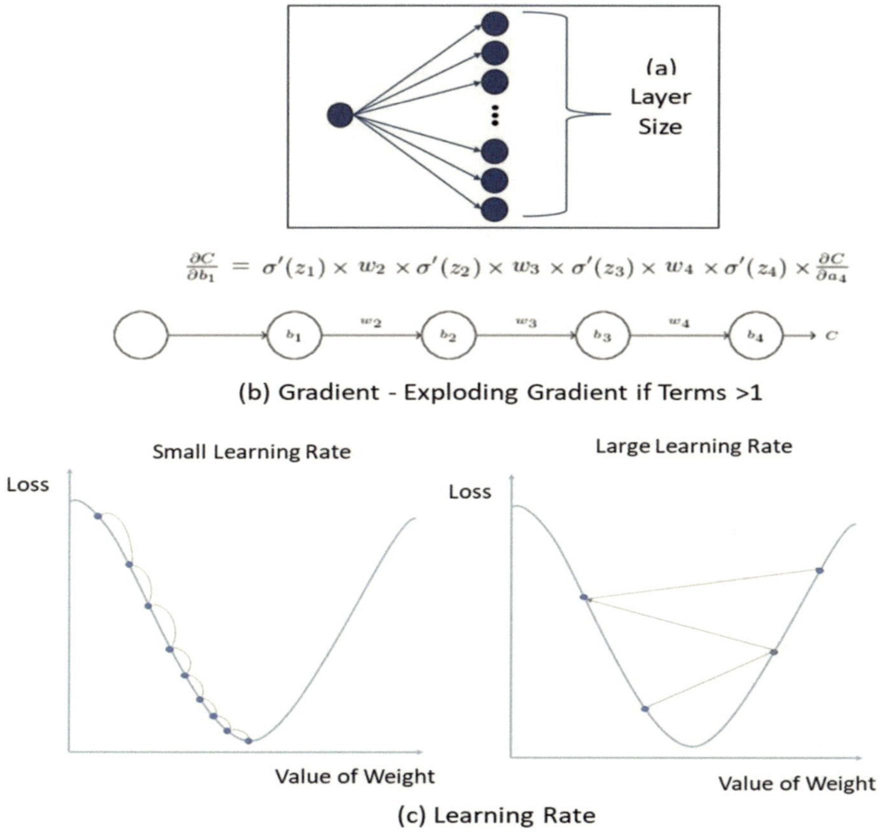


**Figure 3.**
*Deep neural network (DNN) and associated tuning parameters.*

data storage. Tuning the mini-batch size to get the best size for the numerical approximation of the gradient. Tuning the gradient threshold to obtain the best gradient clipping to avoid an "exploding gradient" and the best step size to achieve a timely gradient descent or ascent step. Finally, the tuning of the learning rate is required to achieve the best reward/stopping criteria and learning rate criteria for better convergence. Ref. [16] describes the tuning process for an application of DNN in the design and development of future global navigation and satellite system (GNSS).

### *2.1.4 AI and expert systems*

Earliest example of rule-based expert system was DENDRAL a system for identifying chemical structures developed in the 1960s at Stanford University [17]. DENDRAL was the first system that was called AI and expert system because the decision-making process and problem-solving behavior of organic chemistry were automated to identify unknown organic molecules. Since then, many systems were derived from DENDRAL including MYCIN, REX, MOLGEN, PROSPECTOR, XCON, STEAMER, etc. As an example, MYCIN system was developed in the 1970s to help physicians diagnose meningitis and bacterial infections [18]. As another example, REX system was developed in the 1980s and it was written with the language LIPS from Bell Labs. REX system had advanced the AI and expert system by incorporating rule-based guidance for simple linear regression. The name REX was derived from Regression EXpert, and it was an interface between humans (or users) and statistical software, and an interactive modeling software (IMS). The IMS was created to allow the user interacts with the statistical software more effectively [19].

Since then, the AI and expert systems have undergone rapid evolution. Especially, the COVID pandemic had stimulated private companies to invest in smart and advanced technologies using machine learning and AI, expert systems, cloud computing, and the Internet of Things (IoT) that enable their businesses to make better, more informed decisions in the presence of uncertain environment and fast-changing conditions. As pointed out in [20], currently, ML-AI and expert systems are typically designed and built for specific applications to address specific business or organization needs or technical challenges. They can be classified into two categories, namely, (i) forward chaining ML-AI Expert System (FC/ML-AI-ES) that uses data to predict future events, and (ii) backward chaining ML-AI Expert System (BC/ML-AI-ES) that uses historical data to understand why something occurred. Examples of FC/ML-AI-ES are forecasting inventory demand, or future crop conditions associated with specific geographic areas, etc. Examples of BC/ML-AI-ES are medical diagnostics or troubleshooting complex technical issues in hardware and software systems. A typical ML-AI-ES consists of three primary components, namely, knowledge base (KB), inference engine (IE), and user interface (UI). KB is defined as the data that the ML-AI-ES uses and works with. Modernized KB has automated capabilities that can organize the data and present the data as the user requested it (a.k.a. curate). IE is defined as part of the ML-AI-ES that applies logical rules and related mathematical and/or simulation models (a.k.a. algorithms) that can pull intelligent insights from KB based on user queries. Finally, UI is defined as the means through which a user interacts with KB through a commercial off the shelves software (COTS) platform. **Figure 4** depicts a high-level architecture of a ML-AI-ES [20].

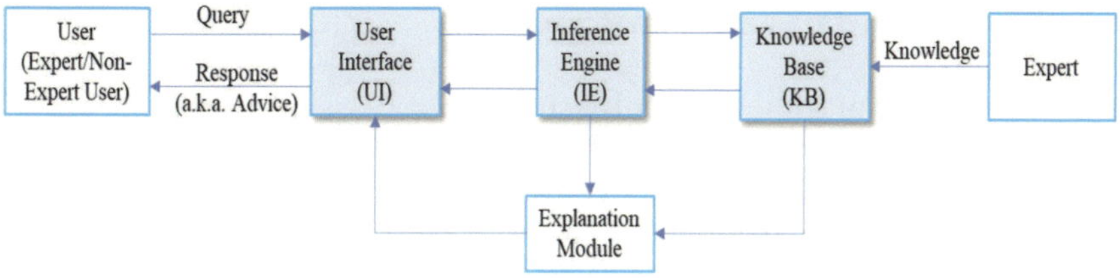


**Figure 4.**
*Typical high-level ML-AI-ES architecture.*

### 2.2 Decision science

Unlike data science, the root of decision science has been found in open literature dated back in the 1930s with an application to economic [21]. As defined by Harvard Chan School of Public Health, Decision Science is the collection of quantitative techniques used to inform decision-making at the individual and population levels[2]. It includes decision analysis, risk analysis, cost–benefit and cost-effectiveness analysis, constrained optimization, simulation modeling, and behavioral decision theory, as well as parts of operations research, microeconomics, statistical inference, management control, cognitive and social psychology, and computer science. With the emergence of ML-AI and digital technologies, decision science ranges from traditional decision theories and analysis to advanced decision theories using emerging decision optimization techniques leveraging game theory, ML-AI, and ML-AI combined with mathematical modeling and simulation (M&S) techniques.

Basically, the traditional decision theory and analysis deal with the reasoning that drives a person's decision, or organization's choice, or a business's decision. In general, the traditional decision theory and analysis consist of three core concepts, including (i) elicitation and interpretation of the decision maker's preferences, (ii) the search of available options, and (iii) the management of uncertainty, risks, and regrets [21–23]. For a large organizations or collective settings involved multiple options associated with different users' needs and interests, the decision-making process is extended to multiple stakeholders. In the 1950s, Von Stackelberg, Nobel laureate John Nash, and Von Neumann are universally credited for their pioneering work on using game theory applied to decision-making process [24–26]. They proposed mathematical models of strategic interaction among rational decision-makers. The latter can be either cooperative or non-cooperative.

## 3. Data and decision sciences (DDS): Recent advances on DDS

As discussed in the previous sections, data and decision sciences (DDS) are interrelated. Data science involves with data collection, data mining, and data analysis. While decision science involves with the process of making decisions through interpretation of the data. But the data interpretation requires data analysis that is a subset of data science. The data analysis is usually conducted by applying mathematical and simulation models and related algorithms for optimizing the risks associated with the decision-making process.

2 https://chds.hsph.harvard.edu/approaches/what-is-decision-science/.

### 3.1 Recent advances in data and decision sciences

As the Industry Revolution 4.0[3] evolves to 5.0, the decision-making process is being challenged by massive data sources and the digitization of the business world along with the rise of environmental uncertainty and risks. Emerging big data analytics, ML-AI, and digitization technologies have allowed for seamless integration of data and decision sciences (DDS). The decision support system (DSS) using big data analytics and ML-AI approach is one of the recent advancements in the integration of DSS (a.k.a. advanced DSS). Along with big data analytics and ML-AI technologies, advanced DSS is a computer-based system that allows for the digitization of the decision-making processes using sophisticated mathematical and simulation models, and advanced optimization techniques. The DSS is designed to allow the decision-makers to make either optimal or satisfactory decisions in the presence of uncertainties. As an example, recently, a group of researchers at Aerospace Corporation has collaborated with North Carolina State University (NCSU), the University of Hawaii at Manoa (UH Manoa), and California State University in Fullerton (CSUF) to develop an advanced DSS tool supporting the development of the optimum acquisition strategy for buying complex space systems with optimum cost and acquisition risk [27–29]. The developed DSS tool leverages multi-criteria decision analysis process, game theory, and advanced optimization techniques to determine the best space system architecture solution and corresponding optimum acquisition strategy to acquire (a.k.a. buy) the system of interest. Finally, as indicated in the table of content, this book has collected a set of chapters addressing the recent advancement of DDS in space, business, medical, and agriculture applications.

## 4. Conclusion

This chapter has provided an overview of the data science and decision science (DDS) and discussed recent advances and DSS applications with a focus on ML-AI technology and its technology enablers. The introductory chapter complements this book's technical content by addressing other DDS topics and applications that are not presented in the chapters presented in this book. It should be pointed out that these book chapters share a common thread of DDS with topics ranges from recent DDS advancements to optimization modeling in decision science and cognitive decision-making process. For each DDS topic, the chapters provide an excellent introduction and background of the DDS problems making these chapters reachable to various scientific and engineering disciplines. Furthermore, for each chapter, the author also takes an effort to (i) discuss technical details associated with the proposed DDS models, and (ii) provide examples to demonstrate the use of the models. This effort from the authors will make their chapters to reach a wide range of readers across many scientific and engineering fields.

We hope that the readers find in this introductory chapter along with book chapters provide intriguing concepts and ideas that would help them solve their DDS problems and a source of ideas for their own work.

---

[3] Industry Revolution 4.0 involves with digitization for automation using cyber physical systems on connected devices, and big data analytics. Industry Revolution 5.0 involves with mass customization and personalization for humans using cognitive computing and human intelligence.

*DOI: http://dx.doi.org/10.5772/intechopen.112546*

**Author details**

Tien M. Nguyen[1,2]

1 California State University in Fullerton (CSUF), California, USA

2 The Aerospace Corporation, USA

*Address all correspondence to: tien.m.nguyen@aero.org

## References

[1] Definition of Data Science. Available from: https://dictionary.cambridge.org/us/dictionary/english/data-science

[2] Definition of Data Science. Available from: https://www.dictionary.com/browse/data-science

[3] Data Science. Available from: https://www.ibm.com/topics/data-science

[4] What's Data Science. Available from: https://ischoolonline.berkeley.edu/data-science/what-is-data-science/

[5] Han J, Kamber M, Pei J. Data Mining Concepts and Techniques. MA, USA: Elsevier Inc, Morgan Kaufmann Publishers; 2012. Available from: http://myweb.sabanciuniv.edu/rdehkharghani/files/2016/02/The-Morgan-Kaufmann-Series-in-Data-Management-Systems-Jiawei-Han-Micheline-Kamber-Jian-Pei-Data-Mining.-Concepts-and-Techniques-3rd-Edition-Morgan-Kaufmann-2011.pdf

[6] Ramageri BM. Data mining techniques and applications. Indian Journal of Computer Science and Engineering. 2010;**1**(4):301-305

[7] Han J. Data mining: Concepts and techniques. In: Department of Computer Science University of Illinois at Urbana-Champaign, chapters 6, Lecture Notes, January 20, 2018. ©2006 Jiawei Han and Micheline Kamber, all rights reserved. Available from: https://www3.cs.stonybrook.edu/~cse634/ch6book.pdf

[8] Fayyad U, Piatetsky-Shapiro G, Smyth P. From Data Mining to Knowledge Discovery in Databases. AI Magazine Volume 17 Number American Association for Artificial Intelligence, © AAAI, 1996. Available from: https://ojs.aaai.org/aimagazine/index.php/aimagazine/article/view/1230/1131

[9] Jamal H. Using Big Data to Predict Stock Market Trends. 2023. Available from: https://medium.datadriveninvestor.com/using-big-data-to-predict-stock-market-trends-312751189d76

[10] Seyedan M, Mafakheri F. Predictive big data analytics for supply chain demand forecasting: Methods, applications, and research opportunities. Journal of Big Data. 2020;**7-53**:1-22, Springer Open. DOI: 10.1186/s40537-020-00329-2

[11] Mendez-Villanueva J, Sopena G, Nguyen TM, Lee CH, Chen Y, Behseta S, et al. Innovative multicarrier broadband waveforms classification using machine learning for future GNSS applications. In: SPACEOPS 2023 Conference Proceedings, the 17th International Conference on Space Operations, 6-10 March 2023, Dubai, United Arab Emirates. Virginia, USA: AIAA

[12] Behseta S. Introduction to Neural Networks and Deep Learning, Lecture Notes Part 1 and Part 2, California State University in Fullerton, Center for Computational and Applied Mathematics (CCAM), 2022. Available from: sbehseta@fullerton.edu

[13] Cunningham JP, Gilja V, Ryu SI, Shenoym KV. Methods for estimating neural firing rates, and their application to brain-machine interfaces. Neural Networks. 2009;**22**(9):1235-1246. DOI: 10.1016/j.neunet.2009.02.004

[14] Gupta P, Balasubramaniam N, Chang H-Y, Tseng F-G, Santra TS. A single-neuron: Current trends and future prospects. Cells. 2020;**9**:1528. DOI: 10.3390/cells9061528. Available from: https://www.ncbi.nlm.nih.gov/pmc/articles/PMC7349798/pdf/cells-09-01528.pdf

[15] Xu J, Chen G, et al. Population-level analysis reveals the widespread occurrence and phenotypic consequence of DNA methylation variation not tagged by genetic variation in maize. Genome Biology. 2019;**20**:243. DOI: 10.1186/s13059-019-1859-0

[16] Nguyen TM, Aguilar J, Lee CH, Paniagua-Rodriguez D, Shen D, Chen G, et al. Onboard HPA pre-distorter using machine learning and artificial intelligence for future GNSS applications. In: 2023 SPIE Conference Proceedings, April 30-May 4, 2023, Orlando, Florida. Bellingham, Washington, USA: SPIE

[17] DENDRAL - Computer Software Expert System. Available from: https://en.wikipedia.org/wiki/Dendral

[18] MYCIN - Backward Chaining Expert System. Available from: https://en.wikipedia.org/wiki/Mycin

[19] Pregibon D, Gale WA. REX: An expert system for regression analysis. In: Proceedings of the 1984 International Association for Statistical Computing, Vienna, Italy. Washington, USA: American Statistical Association; 1984. pp. 242-248

[20] Grant M. AI and Expert Systems: Powering the Future of Business, LeanIX. LeanIX Blogposts. 2022. Available from: https://www.leanix.net/en/blog/artificial-intelligence-expert-systems

[21] Zeuthen F. On the determinateness of the utility function. Review Economic Studies, Oxford University Press. 1937;**4**(3):236-239

[22] Simon H. The Sciences of the Artificial. Massachusetts: MIT Press; 1969

[23] Schlaifer R. Analysis of Decisions under Uncertainty. New York: McGraw-Hill; 1969

[24] Von Stackelberg HF. Market Structure and Equilibrium. 1st edition (translation into English) ed. Vol. 2011. Bazin: Urch & Hill: Springer; 1934

[25] Nash JF. The bargaining problem. In Econometrica. Econometric Society. 1950;**18**(2):155-162

[26] Von Neumann J, Morgenstern O. Theory of Games and Economic Behavior. New Jersey: Princeton University Press; 1953

[27] Nguyen TM, Guillen A, Matsunaga S, Tran HT, Bui TX. "War-Gaming Applications for Achieving Optimum Acquisition of Future Space Systems," a Book Chapter in the book titled "Simulation and Gaming,". London, UK: INTECH-Open Science-Open Minds; 2018. DOI: 10.5772/intechopen.69391

[28] Nguyen TM, Tran HT, Guillen AT, Bui TX, Matsunaga SS. Acquisition war-gaming technique for acquiring future complex systems: Modeling and simulation results for cost plus incentive fee contract. Journal of Mathematics, MDPI - Publisher of Open Access Journals. 2018;**6**(3):1-29. DOI: 10.3390/math6030043. Available from: www.mdpi.com/journal/mathematics

[29] Nguyen TM, Freeze T, Bui TX, Guillen A. Multi-criteria decision theory for enterprise architecture risk assessment: theory, modeling and results. In: Proc. SPIE 11422, Sensors and Systems for Space Applications. Vol. XIII. 2020. p. 114220. DOI: 10.1117/12.2559317

Chapter 2

# Ground-Based HPA Pre-Distorter Using Machine Learning and Artificial Intelligent for Satellite Communication Applications

*Tien M. Nguyen, Charles H. Lee, Sean Cantarini, Xuanyu Huang, Jennifer Gudgel, Chanel Lee, Cristal Gonzalez, Genshe Chen, Dan Shen, John D.T. Nguyen and Khanh D. Pham*

## Abstract

This chapter describes an innovative design and implementation approach of a ground-based pre-distorter framework using machine learning and artificial intelligence (ML-AI) technology for high power amplifier (HPA) pre-distortion. The ML-AI technology enabler proposed is a combined multi-objective reinforce learning-and-adaptive neural network (MORL-ANN) and an operating environment predictor (OEP). The proposed framework addresses the signal distortions caused by a nonlinear HPA on the ground transmitter and a nonlinear HPA located at a satellite communication (SATCOM) transponder (TXDER). The TXDER's HPA is assumed to operate under unknown conditions. The objective is twofold, namely, to demonstrate (i) an advanced decision science technique using ML-AI for future SATCOM applications and (ii) the feasibility of the proposed ground-based ML-AI framework using an end-to-end SATCOM emulator. A new OEP concept using a deterministic and Bayesian approach to improve the MORL-ANN pre-distorter (PD) performance will also be presented.

**Keywords:** satellite communication, ground-based, high power amplifier pre-distorter, machine learning, artificial intelligent, operational environment predictor, signal distortion, high power amplifier

## 1. Introduction

The topic on HPA linearization and the use of machine learning and artificial intelligence (ML-AI) for the high-power amplifier (HPA) linearizer has been investigated in the recent past [1–12]. These works were focused on the linearizer that are usually placed before the HPA and applicable to either a satellite or a ground system with the HPA operating at saturation. This chapter addresses the HPA linearization of an end-to-end satellite system with an uplink (U/L) signal to a satellite transponder

(TXDER) and a downlink signal (D/L) from the TXDER. The proposed ground-based ML-AI HPA pre-distorter concept is intended to place on the ground tracking station and before the ground transmitter's HPA. The novelty of our proposed ground-based ML-AI is to linearize the combined amplitude and phase distortions caused by both the ground and satellite TXDER HPAs.

In practice, a typical SATCOM system includes a U/L and a D/L signals. The U/L signal transmits from a transmit (TX) terminal to a satellite TXDER. The D/L signal transmits from the satellite TXDER to a received (RX) terminal. The TX and RX terminals can be on the ground or an airborne or a navy ship. For the sake of discussion, this chapter assumes it is a fixed ground terminal. For this scenario, the U/L signal is corrupted by the U/L propagation environment including weather, propagation path loss, and U/L radio frequency interferences (RFI). The signal passing through the satellite TXDER is corrupted by transponder processing noise and distortions caused HPA nonlinearity. The D/L signal is also corrupted by the D/L propagation environment including weather, propagation path loss, and D/L RFI. The combined distortion can cause serious Bit Error rate (BER) performance degradation to the received signal on the ground. The use of ML-AI technology to combine data science and decision science (a.k.a. data and decision sciences) can address these challenges. ML-AI can be used to observe the D/L signal amplitude and phase distortions behavior from the ground. It can also be used to predict the amount of distortions for signal compensation before the uplink transmission. In this context, observing the received signal and collecting the received data for predicting the signal distortion behavior is an application of data science. And deciding how much distortion for uplink signal compensation is an application of decision science. Therefore, this is a combined data and decision science technologies.

Through the Industrial Project for Graduate Program in Applied Mathematics (IPGPAM), a collaboration project between CSUF and Intelligent Fusion Technology (IFT) was initiated in 2019 to address this combined data and decision science technologies. During the 2019–2020 academic year, a CSUF team consisting of five graduate students and two faculty members at CSUF was formed to collaborate with the IFT team through this joint industry and university project. This project focused on the advanced mathematical modeling and simulation aspect of the ground-based ML-AI framework for future SATCOM applications. The IFT team provided the end-to-end SATCOM System Model (E2E-SSM) emulator as a platform for demonstrating the newly proposed ground-based ML-AI framework. The CSUF team was responsible for the development of a ground-based HPA pre-distorter (PD) to compensate for the amplitude-to-amplitude and amplitude-to-phase modulation (AM-AM/AM-PM) distortions caused by the HPA nonlinearity and imperfect satellite onboard processing. The problem became more complicated due to unknown operating conditions associated with the satellite system operations, along with the U/L and D/L RFI environment. The RFI can be friendly and unfriendly. Friendly RFI sources are from neighboring satellites using the same RF or the RF near the victim's RF. Unfriendly sources are from adversary jammers. As discussed in [1], for unknown operating conditions, the existing ground-based ML-AI frameworks [2–4] using MORL-ANN require a very large amount of environmental data for all practical operating conditions for training purposes. Thus, with limited training data, trial and error learning-based processes such as MORL-ANN may not be practical in real satellite communication systems where actual operational conditions are varied and at times can be unpredictable. In addition, the use of MORL-ANN described in [2] can potentially run into "bottle-necks" without having proper training data under an unknown

Operational Environment (OE). Also, based on our past simulation results, we have observed that MORL-ANN usually performs very well under a controlled operational environment, where OE conditions, such as system temperatures and propagation loss, are fluctuating predictably and well within the norms. However, when the OE conditions change extensively and rapidly, such as unpredictable RFI power and Total Electron Content (TEC) changing abruptly causing RX signal scintillation, the MORL-ANN might not perform well. As discussed in [1], to address the unknown and uncertain operational environment, our proposed ML-AI framework monitors the received Signal of Interest (SOI) in real time and uses OEP to estimate the operating conditions for reducing uncertainties associated with the observed data before applying MORL-ANN. This proposed technique helps to reduce the amount of data required for training the pre-distorter and avoid the above-mentioned bottleneck.

The CSUF-IFT team has successfully implemented and demonstrated the newly proposed ground-based ML-AI framework addressing satellite TXDER's distortion under unknown HPA operating temperatures and operating Input Back-Off (IPBO). The implemented framework uses the IFT's E2E-SSM emulator as an end-to-end platform [1]. The E2E-SSM emulator includes a sophisticated frequency hopping (FH) satellite modem (modulator-demodulator) and a satellite TXDER model that was verified and validated with existing global broadcasting satellite transponder and global wideband satellite transponder models. This chapter provides a summary of the work performed by the joint CSUF-IFT team. The chapter is organized as follows:

- Section 2 provides a description of the newly proposed ML-AI framework for the unknown operating environment and associated ground-based ML-AI and OEP components.
- Section 3 provides an overview of the E2E-SSM emulator provided by the IFT team.
- Section 4 presents an approach for implementing MORL-ANN for combating AM-AM and AM-PM distortions associated with HPA nonlinearity and unknown operational environment conditions.
- Section 5 discusses approaches for implementing OEP models to reduce uncertainties associated with operational environment conditions.
- Section 6 discusses E2E-SSM simulation results demonstrating the proposed ground-based HPA pre-distorter concept using combined MORL-ANN and OEP for improving performance under unknown TXDER's operational temperature and HPA operating IPBO.
- Section 7 provides the conclusion and way-forward.

## 2. Proposed ground-based ML-AI framework for unknown operating environment

The newly proposed ground-based ML-AI framework for the unknown operating environment was developed by the CSUF team and discussed in [1]. **Figure 1**

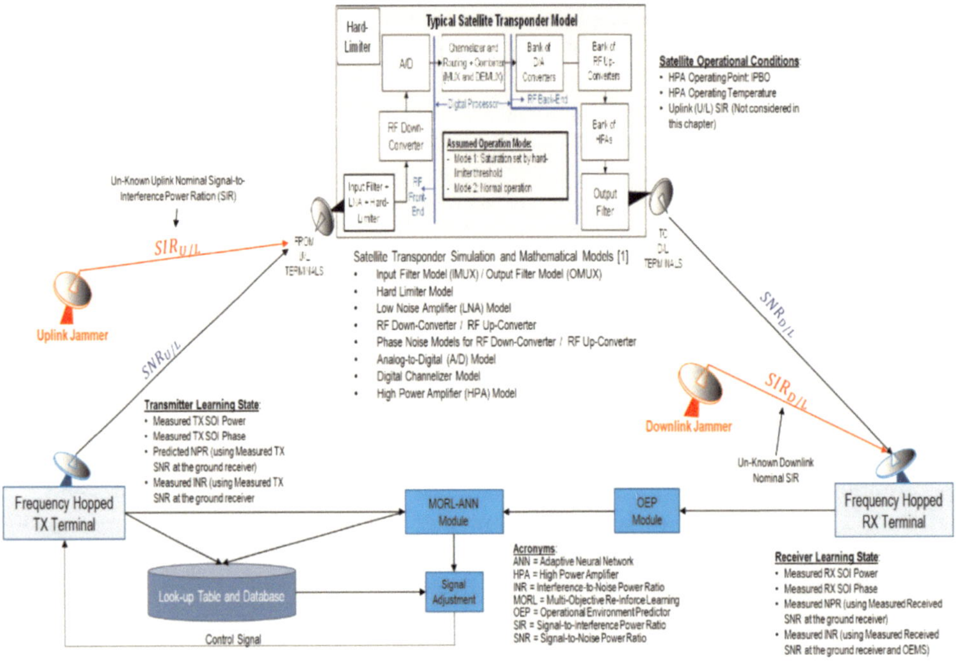


**Figure 1.**
*Proposed ML-AI framework for unknown operating environment.*

illustrates a simplified version of the framework presented in [1]. The ground-based ML-AI framework consists of the following key components:

- FH Transmitted (FH-TX) Terminal: The IFT team developed and provided a MATLAB model capable of simulating square root raised cosine (SRRC) pulse shaping filter QPSK frequency hopping signal at S-band, X-band, and Ka-band frequencies. Section 3 provides a detailed description of this FH-TX model.

- Satellite TXDER Model: IFT also developed and provided a MATLAB wideband satellite TXDER model capable of processing S-band/X-band/Ka-band channelization under imperfect onboard processing conditions. A detailed description of the imperfect onboard processing conditions is also presented in Section 3.

- FH Receiver (FH-RX) Terminal: IFT also supplied the MATLAB FH-RX terminal model. The model is capable of demodulating the hopped frequency signal and recovering the transmitted bits. Section 3 also provides detailed description of this FH-TX model.

- MORL-ANN Module: The CSUF team is responsible for the design and MATLAB implementation of the newly proposed MORL-ANN module. A detailed description and implementation of this model will be discussed in Section 4.

- Operational Environment Predictor (OEP) Module: The CSUF team is also responsible for the design and implementation of the newly proposed OEP module in MATLAB. Section 5 describes the approach for this module.

## 3. E2E-SSM model using FH MODEM

Section 3 provides an overview of the MATLAB models for FH-TX terminal, satellite TXDER model, and FH-RX terminal of the E2E-SSM provided by the IFT team. These MATLAB models serve as the backbone of the proposed ML-AI framework providing an accurate E2E-SSM emulator for generating and collecting SATCOM data at the FH-RX terminal under various operating conditions of interest. The data collection part of this project is thought of as the data science aspect of this problem. For example, what type of data needs to be collected, what actual operating conditions we need to set the E2ESSM emulator, how to arrange the data for the decision-making process, etc.

### 3.1 IFT E2E-SSM using FH MODEM and satellite TXDER

This section presents an overview of the FH modulator–demodulator (MODEM) employed by the emulator and discusses the optimization of processing time allowing real-time simulation. In addition, the training data used for the demonstration of the ground-based ML-AI PD will also be addressed.

**Figure 2(a)–(c)** provides high-level block diagrams of the IFT MATLAB models for the ground FH-TX terminal, satellite TXDER model, and ground FH-RX terminal, respectively. The details of the QPSK modulator and demodulator can be found in [1]. The QPSK modulator can (i) generate a slow frequency hopping or high-frequency hopping rate by controlling the chip rate and (ii) produce a hopped signal with and without SRRC pulse shaping filter. In addition, the MATLAB ground FH-TX terminal

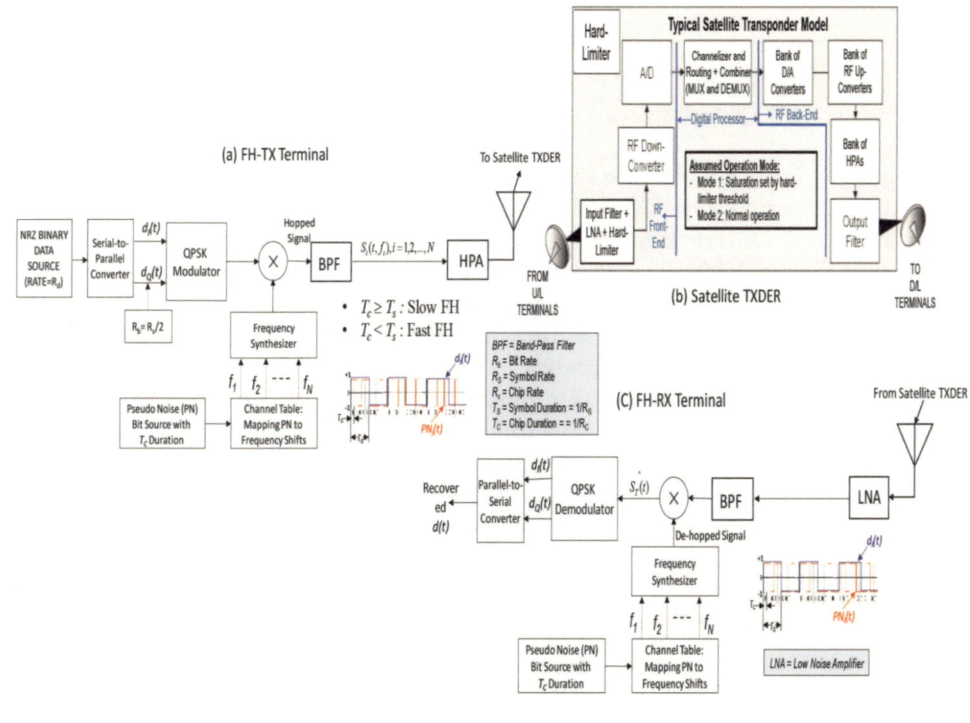


**Figure 2.**
*Block diagrams of IFT MATLAB models: (a) ground FH-TX terminal, (b) satellite transponder, and (c) ground FH-RX terminal.*

also incorporates an HPA model that can accurately generate AM-AM/AM-PM distortions. The MATLAB satellite TXDER model can accurately generate signal distortions caused by imperfect satellite TXDER components. This includes (i) RF-to-IF (intermediate frequency) down-converter, (ii) analog-to-digital converter (ADC), (iii) digital channelizer, (iv) digital-to-analog converter (DAC), (v) IF-to-RF up-converter, and (vi) onboard HPA operation causing AM-AM/AM-PM distortions. The satellite TXDER model is capable of setting practical satellite operating temperatures, IPBO settings, and the amount of distortions caused by imperfect satellite TXDER components. Note that the IPBO setting controls the amount of HPA AM-AM/AM-PM distortions. The ground frequency FH-RX terminal is capable of de-hopping the signal and demodulating the QPSK signal to recover the transmitted data bits and calculate the bit error rate (BER).

In **Figure 2**, let $\boldsymbol{SNR_{NU}}$ be the U/L (i.e., from ground FH-TX terminal to satellite TXDER) signal-to-noise power ratio (SNR), $\boldsymbol{SNR_{DU}}$ be the D/L (i.e., satellite TXDER to FH-RX terminal) SNR, the intermodulation noise (a.k.a. IM noise) caused by the HPA nonlinearity at the TXDER is characterized by $\boldsymbol{C/IM}$ (a.k.a. carrier-to-IM power ratio), and the overall SNR, $\boldsymbol{SNR_0}$, received at the FH-RX terminal, can be shown to have the following form:

$$\frac{1}{SNR_O} = \frac{1}{\left(\frac{1}{SNR_{NU}}\right) + \left(\frac{1}{SNR_{ND}}\right) + \left(\frac{1}{C/IM}\right)} \tag{1}$$

Let us assume that there in a U/L RFI with unknown signal-to-interference power, $\boldsymbol{SIR_U}$, and a D/L RFI with unknown $\boldsymbol{SIR_D}$, and the overall received $\boldsymbol{SNR_0}$ at the FH-RX terminal becomes:

$$\frac{1}{SNR_O} = \frac{1}{\left(\frac{1}{SNR_{NU}}\right) + \left(\frac{1}{SNR_{ND}}\right) + \left(\frac{1}{C/IM}\right) + \left(\frac{1}{SIR_U}\right) + \left(\frac{1}{SIR_D}\right)} \tag{2}$$

Using ML-AI, the FH-RX (see **Figure 2(c)**) observes the overall received $\boldsymbol{SNR_0}$ and predicts the amount of AM-AM and AM-PM distortions caused by the HPA located in the FH-TX terminal (see **Figure 2(a)**) and HPA located in the satellite TXDER (see **Figure 2(b)**). The ground-based ML-AI pre-distorter uses the predicted distortions and pre-distorts the transmitted signal to compensate for the combined AM-AM and AM-PM distortions. As shown in Eq. (2), the distortions depend on the IM at the TXDER. The IM level depends on the HPA operating point, TXDER HPA characteristics, and operating TXDER temperature. The HPA operating point is characterized by the IPBO. In addition, the unknown U/L RFI can change the HPA operating point (i.e., IPBO) causing unknown AM-AM/AM-PM distortions. This chapter investigates the performance of the proposed ground-based ML-AI pre-distorter framework shown in **Figure 1** in the presence of unknown IPBO, HPA AM-AM/AM-PM characteristics, and TXDER operating temperature.

### 3.2 Reducing processing time of existing IFT E2E-SSM

As pointed out in Section 3.1, the signal distortion models caused by imperfect satellite TXDER components with the satellite TXDER include amplitude ripple caused by input/output RF filters, phase noise caused by RF up/down-converters, and quantization noise caused by ADC-DAC, AM-AM/AM-PM distortion effects. The current IFT E2E-SSM model requires excessive processing time, rendering it an inability to support real-time simulation or generate large training data for various operating temperatures and HPA IPBO's. The CSUF graduate students worked on the optimization of the filtering and HPA functions of the IFT E2E-SSM model in MATLAB to (i) reduce processing time which allowed for real-time simulation and (ii) provide for varying HPA operating temperature and IPBO.

### 3.3 Training data for demonstrating proposed ML-AI framework

The CSUF graduate students fine-tuned the E2E-SSM emulator to allow for real-time simulation using the satellite system parameters as shown in **Figure 3(a)**. Using the selected setup, the team generated E2E BER as captured in **Figure 3(b)**. The E2E BER simulation results represent the observed BER performance of a practical FH-QPSK signal under unknown HPA's operating conditions. The unknown HPA's operating conditions considered in the simulation are characterized by the HPA operating temperatures and IPBO as parameters. As specified in **Figure 3(a)**, the HPA operating temperatures and IPBO used in the simulation shown in **Figure 3(b)** are (i) 25°C, 27°C, and 30°C and (ii) IPBO = 0, 5, 7, 10, 13, and 15 dB, respectively.

## 4. Approach for ground-based satellite system operational environment prediction (OEP)

The team proposes two approaches for predicting the operating environment, namely (i) OEP 1—deterministic environmental prediction and (ii) OEP 2—Bayesian environmental prediction. The goal here is to predict the operating conditions, including HPA's temperature and IPBO, based on the measured EbNo and BER values observed by the receiver and pass the results to the MORL-ANN pre-distorter (PD) for training and predicting the amount of AM-AM/AM-PM distortions and compensation.

(a) Satellite TXDER Parameter Settings

- **Operating Parameters:**
  - $bits = 300/ber$
  1. Temperature : 25°C, 27°C, 30°C
  2. bit SNR $(E_b/N_0)$ : 0~9
  3. Bit Error Rate : $10^{-1}$~$10^{-4}$
  4. IPBO (Input Power Back-Off) : 0, 5, 7, 10, 13, 15
  5. Configuration : 1, 2
  6. Channel : [1, 2, 3, 4, 5]; [1, 2, 3, 4]
  7. Band : Ka, Ku, X
  8. Phase Noise : On:1 Off:0
  9. Quantization Noise: On:1 Off:0
  10. HPA Noise : On:1 Off:0
  11. Phase Calibration : On:1 Off:0

(b) E2E BER for Fast FH as a Function of Bit SNR with Satellite System Temperature and IBPO as Parameters

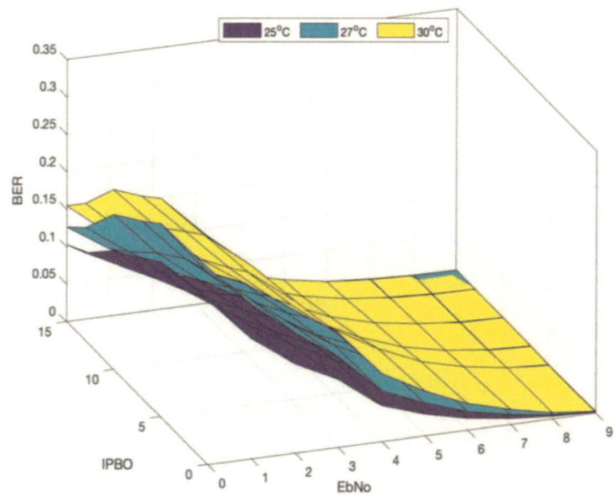


**Figure 3.**
*Generating training data: (a) satellite TXDER parameter setting, (b) E2E BER for fast FH as a function of bit signal-to-noise ratio (EbNo) with satellite system temperature and IPBO as parameters.*

### 4.1 OEP 1: deterministic approach

Given a set of $\{EbNo_i\}_{i=1}^{N_{meas}}$, we measure the corresponding $\{\tilde{BER}_i\}_{i=1}^{N_{meas}}$ and compute the mean square error (MSE) based on the previously generated data set using:

$$MSE(T, IPBO) = \sum_{i=1}^{N_{meas}} \left(BER(EbNo_i, T, IPBO) - \tilde{BER}_i\right)^2 \tag{3}$$

The goal is to choose the best temperature $T^*$ and $IPBO^*$ that minimizes the least mean square error.

### 4.2 OEP 2: Bayesian approach

This approach uses the existing MATLAB function "*fitcnb*," which fits a native Bayes classifier model. The native Bayes classifier model uses simple probabilistic classifiers based on Bayes' theorem with strong but naïve independence assumptions between the features of the data.

## 5. Approach for ground-based MORL-ANN PD

The proposed ground-based MORL-ANN PD (or simply PD) can be implemented using a deep deterministic policy gradient (DDPG) technology enabler or a combined DDPG with deep-Q learning network (DQN). This section describes these two implementation approaches.

### 5.1 PD implementation using DDPG

The goal for the MORL-ANN PD is to pre-distort the TX signal such that the received (RX) signal is identical to the transmit (TX) signal [3, 4]. The ML-AI technology enabler that is available from MATLAB is the DDPG [5–8]. The DDPG is suitable for the MORL-ANN training and prediction that involves tuning the parameters of a deep neural network (DNN). As depicted in **Figure 4**, DDPG is an actor-critic network that is the heart of the proposed ML-AI framework, where the actor observes the received data and decides on required actions, and the critic judges the actions and rewards or penalizes the actions using a pre-defined loss function. The word "deep" in DDPG represents the DNN with two or more hidden layers,

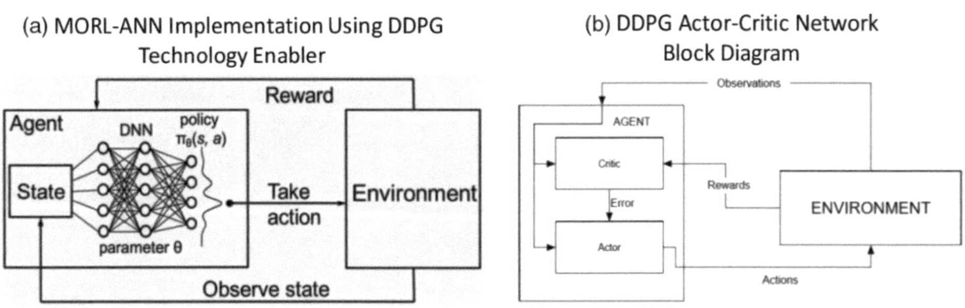


**Figure 4.**
*(a) MORL-ANN implementation using DDPG and (b) DDPG actor-critic network block diagram.*

"deterministic" means that there is only one-output, "policy" means that the PD has a policy for deciding an action, and "gradient" means that the PD uses gradient of the loss function to update previous values.

DNN is a structure that consists of a sequence of functions (layers), which takes in our state (or a state-action pair) and returns to us an action (or our expected reward). Here, the MORL training occurs in episodes that consist of k steps. A step is a process whereby an action is generated by the agent. The action is processed by the environment, and the resulting reward is returned to the agent. For our MORL-ANN implementation, an episode consists of a single step. The MORL-ANN algorithm is expressed as follows:

$$\text{Form Policy Gradient } \nabla J(\theta): \text{ where } J(\theta) = E\left[\text{Reward}_{\text{Episode}}\right] \quad (4)$$

where our neural networks are determined by a parameter vector $\theta$ representing system operating conditions, such as operating temperature and IPBO

- Calculate $\nabla J(\theta)$: using Monte Carlo Methods

- Perform a gradient ascent step:

$$\theta \leftarrow \theta + \ \nabla J, \text{ where } 0 < \ < 1 \text{ is the learning rate.} \quad (5)$$

The proposed DNN tuning requires fine-tuning the training parameters, involving:

- Layer size: layer size refers to the output sizes of the fully-connected layers in the networks. It is a vector of length 2.

- Mini batch size: when performing a gradient ascent step for DDPG, we approximate the policy gradient over k data points using Monte Carlo methods. Here, k is called the mini batch size.

- Gradient threshold: when the policy gradient's Euclidean norm exceeds the gradient threshold, we rescale it so that its Euclidean norm is the gradient threshold. This controls the learning speed in the gradient ascent step.

The "Reward" is defined as the error of the signal amplitudes and error of the signal phase after the HPA is expressed in negative values. For tuning, we take the L2 norm between the post-HPA PD signal and the original transmitted signal from the ground FH-TX terminal. For final training, we will use the L2 norm between the "SlidingBucket" normalized signals for greater accuracy. The "SlidingBucket" is an algorithm that our team developed to emulate the automatic gain control (AGC) to maintain the IPBO level. The IPBO level is updated depending on the selected AGC loop time response (i.e., update rate). The CSUF graduate students[1] spent a tremendous amount of time fine-tuning the training parameters and found an optimum set of training parameters for the final simulation run. The simulation results are shown in Section 6.2.

[1] Sean Cantarini was the lead of the graduate student team to fine tune the MORL-ANN PD.

### 5.2 PD implementation using combined DDPG and deep-Q learning

The CSUF graduate student team[1] proposed a hybrid concept to use the MATLAB's DDPG for designing a good MORL-ANN PD and then deep-Q learning network (DQN) to make further corrections. **Figure 5** illustrates the proposed concept. The DQN uses a single, smaller neural network. It uses much less memory and can feasibly take many small, discrete actions due to the agent's smaller size, thereby more efficient for stabilization purposes. Thus, using the initial state prediction provided by OEP concerning the HPA operating temperature and IPBO, the DQN agent will take a much shorter time due to the small number of steps required to reach a desirable stable state. Combining DQN with DPPG can improve the training time and enhance the MORL-ANN PD performance.

## 6. Simulation results

This section provides the simulation results obtained from the IFT E2E-SSM emulator using the training data presented in Section 3.3 to demonstrate the ground-based ML-AI concept to compensate for the AM-AM/AM-PM distortions caused by the ground terminal's HPA and satellite TXDER's HPA in the presence of unknown operating conditions.

### 6.1 Ground-based OEP simulation results

This section presents the simulation results for proposed OEP using deterministic and Bayesian approaches.

#### *6.1.1 OEP simulation results for deterministic approach: OEP 1*

**Figure 6** shows the results for the deterministic prediction simulation results for a measured BER at 0.001. The results show that the predicted operating conditions with the lowest error are a temperature of 27°C with an IPBO value of 5. **Figure 6** presents the simulation results for the deterministic prediction when the measured BER is at 0.01 with a number of measured EbNo values of 2. These results show that only 35 out of 100 trials correctly predict both the operating temperature and IPBO.

**Figures** 7 and **8** capture the simulation results for the deterministic prediction at a measured BER of 0.01 and 0.001, with a numerical measured value of 2 and 4, respectively. For the measured BER of 0.001, the results show that 96 out of 100 trials correctly predicted both operating temperature and IPBO. Thus, when the number of

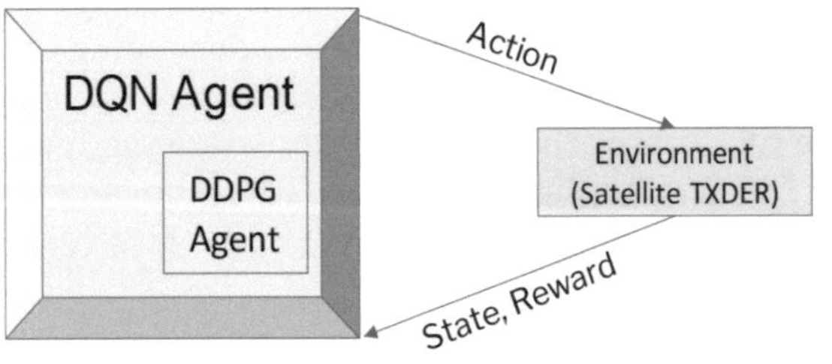


**Figure 5.**
*MORL-ANN implementation using combined DDPG-and-DQN.*

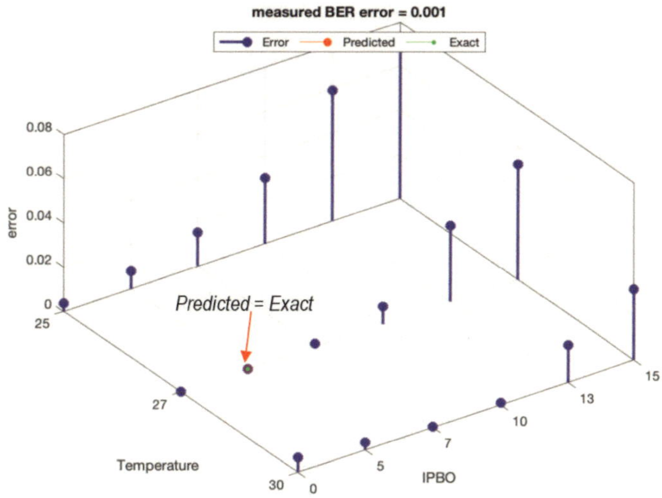


**Figure 6.**
*Deterministic prediction simulation results for BER = 0.001.*

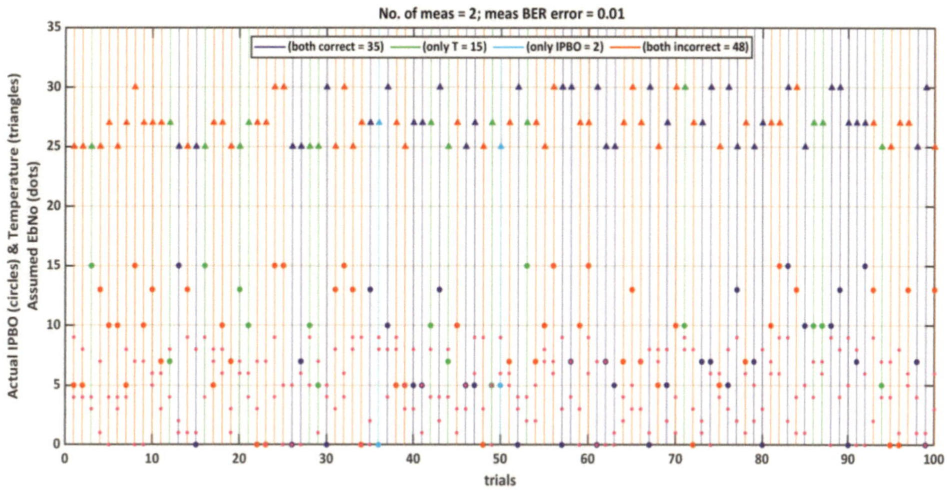


**Figure 7.**
*Deterministic prediction simulation results for BER = 0.01 with number of measured EbNo values of 2.*

measured EbNo increases, the probability of correctly identifying the operating conditions improves.

### *6.1.2 OEP simulation results for Bayesian approach: OEP 2*

**Figure 9** provides the results on the probability of classification as a function of EbNo and BER obtained from the Naïve Bayesian classification model. **Figure 9** shows that the probability of classification is at its highest, about 0.3, when BER = 0.3 and operating system temperature and IPBO are at 27°C and 15 dB, respectively.

**Figure 9** presents simulation results using the Naïve Bayesian prediction approach.

The results were obtained using four measured BER values for predicting HPA's operating temperature and IPBO. **Figure 10** shows that the highest predicted

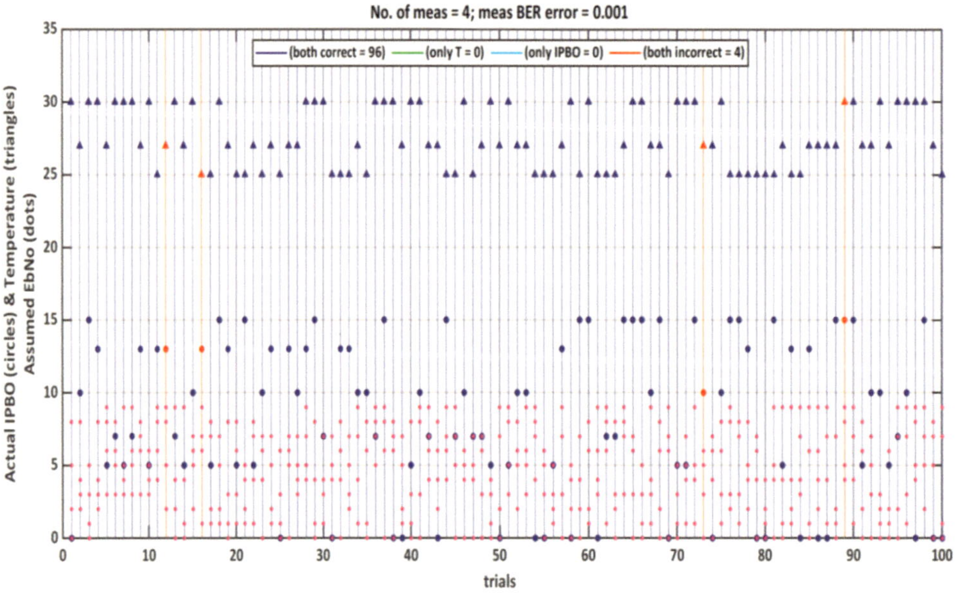


**Figure 8.**
*Deterministic prediction simulation results for BER = 0.001 with number of measured EbNo values of 4.*

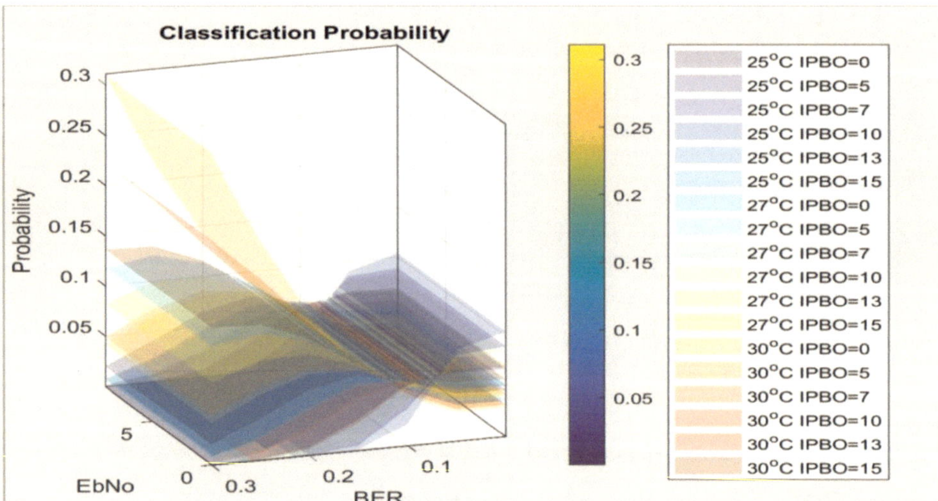


**Figure 9.**
*Probability of classification.*

probability sum value is for 25°C with an IPBO value of 10, while the actual value is at 25°C with an IPBO value of 13.

**Table 1** summarizes the results for comparison between the two OEP approaches. As shown in **Table 1**, the deterministic approach achieves the best performance when the number of measurements is 4 or more and the BER is at 10E-3 or less. However, for the Bayesian classification approach, the probability of classification is inconclusive when increasing the number of measured BERs. Our team expects that the use of a "Kernel" can improve the probability of classification of the operating environment.

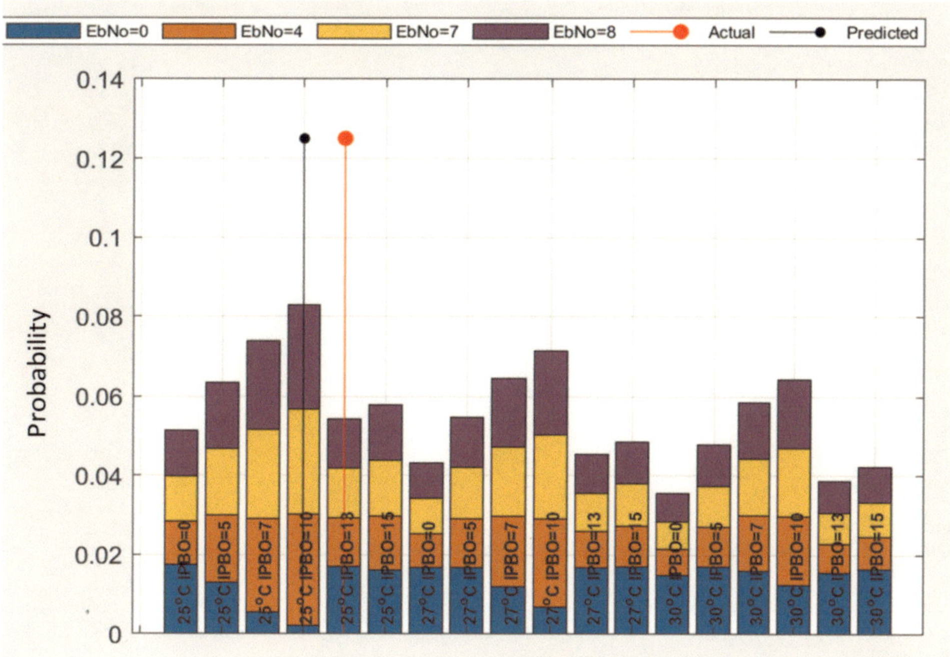


**Figure 10.**
*Probability of classification results for EbNo ranging from 0 to 8 dB.*

| | **BER error = $10^{-3}$** | | | **BER error = $10^{-2}$** | | | **BER error = $10^{-1}$** | | |
|---|---|---|---|---|---|---|---|---|---|
| *Deterministic* | | | | | | | | | |
| Number of meas | 2 | 3 | 4 | 2 | 3 | 4 | 2 | 3 | 4 |
| Both correct | 87 | 92 | 96 | 35 | 40 | 54 | 8 | 8 | 7 |
| Just temperature | 2 | 0 | 0 | 15 | 12 | 9 | 31 | 37 | 36 |
| Just IPBO | 1 | 0 | 0 | 2 | 7 | 3 | 14 | 7 | 16 |
| Both incorrect | 10 | 8 | 3 | 48 | 41 | 34 | 47 | 48 | 41 |
| *Naïve Bayesian classification* | | | | | | | | | |
| Number of meas | 2 | 3 | 4 | 2 | 3 | 4 | 2 | 3 | 4 |
| Both correct | 4 | 3 | 5 | 4 | 2 | 2 | 4 | 2 | 6 |
| Just temperature | 40 | 28 | 29 | 29 | 27 | 31 | 33 | 28 | 36 |
| Just IPBO | 6 | 6 | 3 | 1 | 7 | 8 | 9 | 5 | 5 |
| Both incorrect | 50 | 63 | 63 | 66 | 64 | 59 | 54 | 65 | 53 |

**Table 1.**
*Deterministic vs. Bayesian classification.*

### 6.2 Ground-based MORL-ANN Predistorter simulation results

**Figure 11** shows the simulation results for MORL-ANN PD using MATLAB's DDPG algorithm with the initial operating conditions prediction provided by OEP 1 approach. The results show that AM/AM (signal power curve) and AM/PM (signal

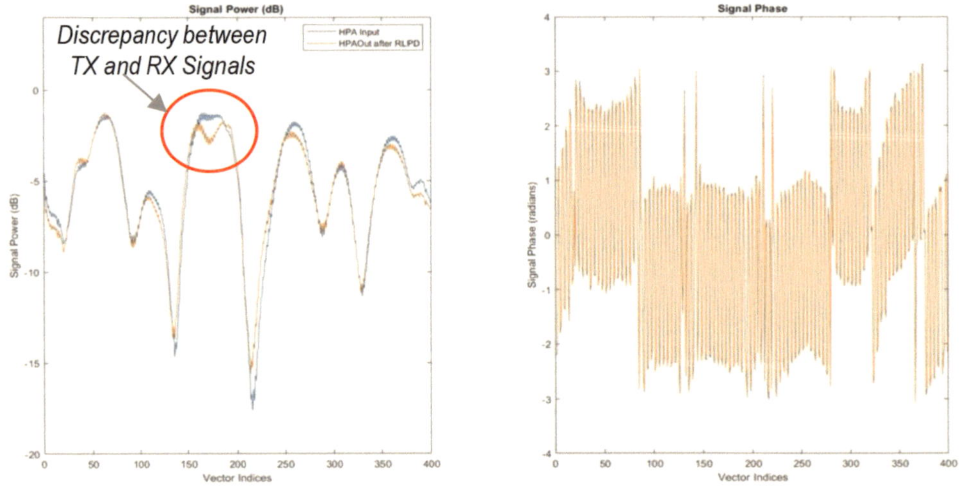


**Figure 11.**
*MORL-ANN PD simulation results using existing DDPG in MATLAB.*

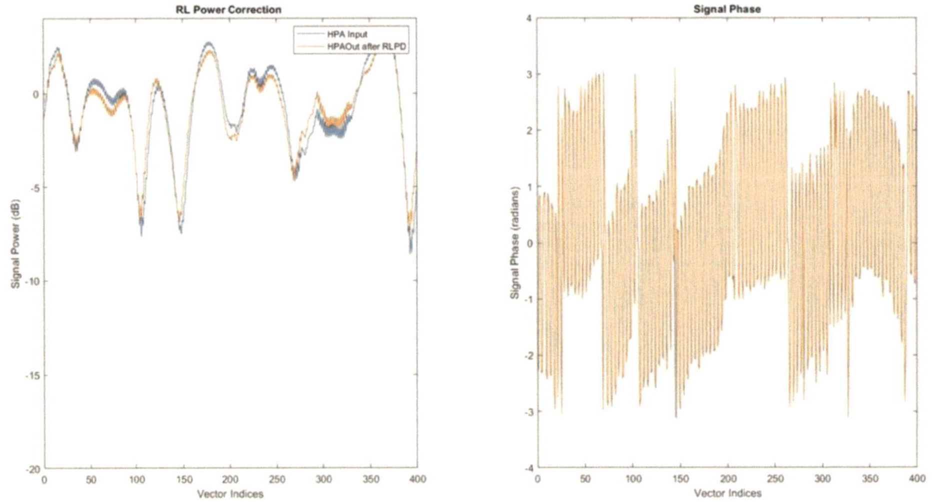


**Figure 12.**
*MORL-ANN PD simulation results using the combined DDPG and DQN in MATLAB.*

phase curve) between the TX and RX signals are in good agreement, i.e., the PD provides an accurate prediction of AM/AM-AM/PM distortions and compensates for them. This means any inaccuracy associated with OEP eventually corrects itself through the MORL-ANN training and prediction processes. The results shown in **Figure 11** also show that there is a slight disagreement between the actual and predicted AM/AM distortion causing a discrepancy between the TX and RX signals between the Vector Index 150 and 200.

Our team has investigated the problem and learned that when using the combined deep Q-learning neural network (DQN) and DDPG during the learning and training process, the MORL-ANN PD performs better with the use of OEP. **Figure 12** presents the simulation results using the combined DQN-DPPG approach for mitigating the AM/AM discrepancy between the TX and RX signals.

Based on the MATLAB implementation, our team has learned that the use of DDPG allowed to use a single, smaller neural network, so it uses much less memory. This implementation can feasibly take many small, discrete actions (due to the agent's smaller size), so it is more convenient for stabilization. However, given a bad initial state, the agent will take a long time (many steps) or never reach a desirable state. Thus, for our problem, we recognize that the DDPG can train faster and typically produces better results than DQN alone.

## 7. Conclusion and way forward

This chapter provides a summary of the work performed by the CSUF-IFT team on an Industrial Collaboration Project during the 2019–2020 academic year. The project described in this chapter focuses on the MATLAB implementation and demonstration of the novel ground-based ML-AI framework presented in **Figure 1**. The proposed MATLAB implementation employs MORL-ANN combined with a deterministic OEP for predicting and compensating signal distortions caused by the ground terminal transmitter' HPA and satellite TXDER's HPA, and imperfect onboard signal processing. Preliminary results presented here have demonstrated the (i) feasibility of the proposed deterministic OEP for reducing operating environment uncertainties associated with unknown satellite TXDER's HPA operating temperature and IPBO, and (ii) use of MORL-ANN using DPPG and MORL-ANN using combined DQN-DPPG for compensating of AM-AM/AM-PM distortions caused by combined ground station's HPA and satellite TXDER's HPA.

Considering the preliminary OEP simulation results, it has been shown that the current proposed environment predictor using Bayesian approach is inconclusive. The CSUF-IFT team continues to investigate the use of ML-AI technology to improve the Bayesian OEP.

Last but not least, the chapter has proposed an approach to combine the data science and decision science to solve a challenging problem in satellite communication in the presence of unknown operational conditions. Our team has developed an end-to-end SATCOM system model (E2E-SSM) emulator to generate a large amount of data for various practical operational conditions, including unknown IPBO, system operating temperature, HPA's AM-AM/AM-PM characteristics, and SNR. Using the data obtained from the emulator, the team has also developed an innovative ML-AI framework to (i) learn the behavior of amplitude and phase distortions of the received downlink signal, (ii) predict the amount of amplitude and phase of the transmitted uplink signal, and (iii) and adjust them accordingly for negating the effects of the HPA nonlinearity on the end-to-end communication signals. Our simulation results presented in this chapter has demonstrated the feasibility of these proposed combined technologies. Our team is also investigating the use of the proposed ML-AI pre-distorter for future Global Navigation Satellite System (GNSS) applications. The results of these investigations will be reported in the near future.

## Acknowledgements

IFT was awarded the SBIR Phase 1 in 2019, and contract number was FA9453-18-P-0233 from AFRL, entitled "Hybrid Low-Cost Predistortion Solutions for Next Generation Satellite Transponder," as the prime contractor. The results presented in this chapter were done during Phase 1 (toward the end of Phase 1) through the Industrial Project for Graduate Program in Applied Mathematics (IPGPAM), which is a joint collaboration project between CSUF and IFT. Recently, IFT was awarded the SBIR Phase 2 contract, Contract No. FA9453-21-C-0539 from AFRL. Additionally, CSUF was awarded a subcontract from IFT, Subcontract Number: IFT083-02. The subcontract focused on maturing the proposed ML-AI technology enabler and OEP for future GNSS applications. The paper was cleared for public release, Case No. AFRL-2022-5077. Any opinions, findings, conclusions, or recommendations expressed in this material are those of the authors and do not necessarily reflect the views of AFRL.

## Notes/thanks/other declarations

The authors want to thank Maria Rios of IFT for her careful review of the paper. The first author wishes to thank his wife, Thu-Hang Nguyen, for her enormous patience and boundless support during the preparation of this chapter.

## Author details

Tien M. Nguyen[1,2]*, Charles H. Lee[1]*, Sean Cantarini[1,3], Xuanyu Huang[1,3], Jennifer Gudgel[1,3], Chanel Lee[1,3], Cristal Gonzalez[1,3], Genshe Chen[4], Dan Shen[4], John D.T. Nguyen[4] and Khanh D. Pham[5]

1 California State University in Fullerton (CSUF), Fullerton, California, USA

2 The Aerospace Corporation, USA

3 CSUF, Applied Mathematics, USA

4 Intelligent Fusion Technology, Inc (IFT), Germantown, Maryland, USA

5 Air Force Research Laboratory, New Mexico, USA

*Address all correspondence to: tmnguyen57@fullerton.edu; charleshlee@fullerton.edu

## References

[1] Nguyen TM. Machine learning and artificial intelligent addressing satellite transponder distortions. In: 2020 IEEE Green Energy and Smart Systems Conference Proceedings, November 2-3, 2020, Long Beach, CA. Institute of Electrical and Electronics Engineers (IEEE); 2020. IEEE #: CFP2031Y-USB. ISBN: 9781728187433. Available from: https://www.proceedings.com/57020.html

[2] Ferreira P, Paffenroth R, Wyglinski A, Hackett T, Bilén S, Reinhart R, et al. Reinforcement learning for satellite communications: From LEO to deep space operations. IEEE Communications Magazine. 2019;**57**(5): 70-75. DOI: 10.1109/MCOM.2019.1800796

[3] Lu J, Li L, Nguyen J, Shen D, Tian X, Chen G, et al. Machine learning based adaptive predistorter for high power amplifier linearization. In: 2019 IEEE Cognitive Communications for Aerospace Applications Workshop (CCAAW). Available from: https://ieeexplore.ieee.org/document/8904896

[4] Lun L, Nguyen J, Lu J, Shen D, Tian X, et al. An effective satellite transponder linearization method using a physics-based predistorter. In: Proc. SPIE 11017, Sensors and Systems for Space Applications XII, 110170G (29 July 2019). 2019. DOI: 10.1117/12.2520482. Available from: https://www.spie.org/Publications/Proceedings/Paper/10.1117/12.2520482?origin_id=x4325&start_volume_number=11000&SSO=1

[5] Sutton RS, Barto AG. Reinforcement Learning: An Introduction. MIT Press; 2018. Available from: https://mitpress.mit.edu/9780262039246/reinforcement-learning/

[6] Deep Deterministic Policy Gradient Agents. Mathworks, Re-Inforcement Learning website

[7] Reinforcement Learning Agents. Mathworks, Re-Inforcement Learning website

[8] Everything You Need to Know About Adaptive Neural Networks. Allerin Blog

[9] Beale MH et al. MATLAB Neural Network ToolboxTM7. Mathworks website

[10] Nguyen TM, Yoh J, Lee C, Tran HT, Johnson DM. Modeling of HPA and HPA linearization through a predistorter: Global broadcasting service applications. IEEE Transaction on Broadcasting. 2003; **49**(2):132-141. DOI: 10.1109/TBC.2003.813650. Available from: https://ieeexplore.ieee.org/document/1208428

[11] Borel A, Barzdenas V, Vasjanov A. Linearization as a solution for power amplifier imperfections: A review of methods. Electronics. 2021;**10**:1073. DOI: 10.3390/electronics10091073

[12] Feng X. Efficient baseband digital predistortion techniques for linearizing power amplifier by taking into account nonlinear memory effect [PhD thesis]. l'Université de Nantes; 2015. Available from: https://hal.science/tel-01206266/document

Section 2

# Recent DDS Advancements in Business, Medical, and Agriculture Applications

Chapter 3

# Perspective Chapter: Application of Monte Carlo Methods in Strategic Business Decisions

*Chioma Ngozi Nwafor*


## Abstract

Some strategic business problems cannot be expressed in analytical forms and, in most cases, are difficult to define in a deterministic manner. This chapter explores the use of probabilistic modelling using Monte Carlo methods in the modelling of decision problems. The focus is on using Monte Carlo simulation to provide a quantitative assessment of uncertainties and key risk drivers in business decisions. Using an example based on hypothetical data, we illustrate decision problems where uncertainties make simulation modelling useful to obtain decision insights and explore alternative choices. We will explore how to propagate uncertainty in input decision variables to get a probability distribution of the output(s) of interest.


**Keywords:** Monte Carlo methods, probability distributions, decision variable, probabilistic and stochastic modelling, decision analytics

## 1. Introduction

Many critical business challenges involve decision-making under uncertainty. Some examples of decision-making under uncertainty in the business world include decision to introduce a new product, capital budgeting decisions, strategic decisions to increase net profit and decisions to grant loans by a financial institution. Accounting for these sources of uncertainty and balancing the objectives of the business can be very challenging. This chapter discusses probabilistic modelling using Monte Carlo methods in modelling of decision problems. The focus is on using Monte Carlo simulation to provide a quantitative assessment of uncertainties and critical risk drivers in business decisions. Given adequate data and reasonable assumptions, probabilistic modelling techniques, such as Monte Carlo analysis can be viable statistical tools for analyzing uncertainty in business decisions. To make the most out of probabilistic modelling using Monte Carlo methods, executives must combine all available insights about the relevant uncertainties and their impact on their decisions.

Literature uses the terms probabilistic and stochastic modelling interchangeably. It is essential to provide a brief definition of these terms. Probabilistic modelling is a statistical technique used to consider the impact of random events or uncertainty in predicting the potential occurrence of future outcomes [1, 2]. Probabilistic models incorporate probability distributions into the model of an event or phenomenon. These models are hinged on the premise that we rarely know everything about a situation. Therefore, there is always an element of randomness or uncertainties to consider. On the other hand, stochastic modelling forecasts the probability of various outcomes under different conditions using random variables [3]. The word stochastic comes from the Greek word *stokhazesthai*, meaning to aim or guess. Essentially, a stochastic model estimates probability distributions of potential outcomes by accounting for random variation in the input variables. Some examples of stochastic models include Monte Carlo simulation and Markov chain models amongst others [3]. These models use probability distributions to account for uncertainties in the input variables. In a strict sense, stochastic modelling is an area of probability and statistics used in decision-making under uncertainties. Like probability modelling, stochastic modelling presents data and predicts outcomes that account for certain levels of unpredictability or randomness. In this chapter, we use probabilistic and stochastic modelling interchangeably because both models are based on probability or the fact that randomness plays a role in predicting future events. The stochastic approach we will use is the Monte Carlo simulation method.

Using an example based on hypothetical data, we illustrate decision problems where uncertainties make probabilistic/stochastic modelling useful to obtain decision insights and explore alternative choices. We will explore how to propagate uncertainty in input decision variables to get a probability distribution of the output(s) of interest. The rest of the chapter is structured as follows. Section 2 discusses probability distributions and the distributions used in the example (Normal, Lognormal, Bernoulli, and Triangular distributions). Section 3 explores how to deal with uncertainty using a probabilistic/stochastic model. Section 4 provides an application of Monte Carlo methods in making business decisions, while Section 5 is the conclusion.

## 2. Probability modelling and Monte Carlo simulation

Business uncertainty is when the outcome of a strategic business decision is unclear, often due to a lack of information or knowledge about the business environment. The conventional approach to strategic business decisions assumes that executives can predict the future of any business accurately enough to choose a clear strategic direction for it by applying standard deterministic spreadsheet models. Such deterministic models allow you to calculate a future event precisely, without the involvement of randomness. However, deterministic models do not account for the fact that the business environments are complex and constantly changing. For instance, deterministic models assume that known average rates with no random deviations can be applied to the broader population. For example, if 10,000 businesses each have a 95% chance of surviving another year, we can be reasonably confident that 9500 businesses will indeed survive.

In contrast, probability models using Monte Carlo simulation allow for random variations due to uncertainties in the parameters or limited sample size for which it may not be reasonable to apply average rates. For example, consider a sample of 10,000 businesses in the U.K. with each having a probability of 0.7 of surviving another year. The average number of companies that may survive another year will be $10{,}000 \times 0.7 = 7000$. However, due to the limited sample size of the population, there will be random variations, and a probabilistic description of the population at the end of the year would be preferable. We would use a probability distribution to describe the population in this case. The probability distribution provides the probabilities of having zero survivors, one survivor, two survivors, and more survivors at the end of the year. A probability distribution is given for the number of businesses that will survive another year and not just an average number.

When the future is genuinely uncertain, a deterministic approach is at best marginally helpful and very dangerous, given that underestimating uncertainty can lead to strategies that neither defend a company against the threats nor take advantage of the opportunities that higher levels of uncertainty provide. Major analytical tools such as probabilistic modelling using Monte Carlo simulation and game theory, amongst others, offer enormous opportunities for business executives working in industries facing significant uncertainties. What follows is a discussion of probabilistic modelling using Monte Carlo simulation and an analysis of the probability distributions used in this chapter.

We can categorize data for modelling business decisions into **input data** (explanatory data) and **output data** (predicted/outcome data). A major aspect of dealing with business uncertainty is using quantitative methods to model uncertainty. For example, a firm's net profit 1 year from today is uncertain. We know that a firm's net profit 1 year from today is a function of many uncertain input variables, including the demand for the company's goods/services, the cost of goods sold and tax rate, amongst others. Some of these input variables are outside the control of the decision-maker. Probability models can be used to propagate uncertainty in the input variables. Probability modelling uses probability distributions of input assumptions to calculate the probability distribution for chosen output metrics/summary measures [4]. It is important to remember that uncertainty in business decisions is unavoidable because real-world situations cannot be perfectly measured, modelled or predicted. As a result, business decision-makers face significantly complex problems compounded by varying levels of uncertainty. If uncertainty has not been well acknowledged, potential complications arise in the process of decision-making. Decision-makers often want to know the impact of certain business decisions on their bottom line, how much the trade-off between alternative actions reduces their potential profit and the possible consequences of decisions.

Monte Carlo simulation allows executives to see all the possible outcomes of their decisions and assess the impact of risk, thus, allowing for better decision-making under uncertainty. Probability distributions are a realistic way of describing uncertainty in variables. Monte Carlo methods are defined as statistical approaches to provide approximate solutions to complex optimization or simulation problems by using random sequences of numbers [5–7]. The Monte Carlo method performs analysis by building models of possible results via substituting a range of values—a probability distribution—for any factor with inherent uncertainty. The algorithm then calculates results repeatedly, each time using a different set of random values from the probability functions. In other words, values are sampled at random during a Monte Carlo simulation from the input probability distributions and each set of samples is called an iteration. The resulting outcome from that sample is recorded. Each iteration produces different values for the input assumptions fed into the model. Monte Carlo simulation could involve thousands or tens of thousands of recalculations before producing a probability distribution of possible outcomes.

Using probability distributions allow variables to have different probabilities of different outcomes occurring. Probabilistic modelling using the Monte Carlo method tells you what could happen and how likely it is to happen. What follows is a brief discussion of the common probability distributions used in decision analytics.

## 2.1 Common probability distributions in business decision making

Organizations and governments use mathematical models, optimization algorithms and other tools in their decision-making to achieve strategic organizational goals. However, essential variables such as future sales, future material costs, etc., are often uncertain. In reality, a plan that promises high performance, in theory, can go wrong when assumptions change or prove false, or we encounter unanticipated events such as regional wars or events like the COVID-19 global pandemics. Probabilistic modelling using Monte Carlo simulation methods can assist decision-makers in making strategic business decisions in the face of uncertainties. Probability models represent events as probabilities rather than certainties, using probability distributions to increase expected returns or reduce downside risk. The main goals of this section are to present a brief review of distribution fitting and a discussion of the following probability distributions - *Normal*, *Lognormal*, *Bernoulli* and *Triangular distributions*. We start with a discussion of probability distribution and then discuss each probability distribution mentioned above in turn below.

### *2.1.1 Review of distribution fitting*

Distribution fitting is used to select a statistical distribution that best fits a data set. Examples of statistical distributions include the normal, lognormal, Bernoulli and triangular distributions. A distribution characterizes a variable when the distribution conditions match those of the variable. The maximum likelihood estimation (MLE) method estimates the distribution's parameters from a data set. Once the estimation is complete, you use goodness of fit techniques to help determine which distribution fits your data best. Distributions are defined by parameters. These parameters define the distribution. There are four parameters used in distribution fitting: *location*, *scale*, *shape* and *threshold*. The ***location parameter*** of distribution indicates where the distribution lies along the x-axis (the horizontal axis). The ***scale parameter*** of distribution determines how much spread there is in the distribution. The larger the scale parameter, the more spread there is in the distribution. The smaller the scale parameter, the less spread there is in the distribution. On the other hand, the ***shape parameter*** allows the distribution to take different shapes. The larger the shape parameter, the more the distribution tends to be skewed to the left. The smaller the shape parameter, the more the distribution tends to be skewed to the right. At the same time, the ***threshold parameter*** defines the minimum value of the distribution along the x-axis. The distribution cannot have any values below this threshold.

### *2.1.2 The normal distribution*

The normal distribution is the single most important distribution in statistics. The normal distribution is a continuous distribution characterized by its mean and standard deviation. Therefore, we say that the normal distribution is a *two-parameter* distribution. The normal curve shifts to the right or left by changing the mean. If the standard deviation is changed, the curve spreads out more or less. The possible values of the normal distribution range over the entire number line - from minus infinity (i.e., $-\infty$) to plus infinity (i.e., $+\infty$). Random variables from the normal distribution form the foundation of probabilistic modelling. This distribution is also known as the Bell Curve, and it occurs naturally in many circumstances. For example, the normal distribution is seen in tests like the general certificate of secondary education (GCSE) or National 5 examination in the U.K., where most students will score the average grade (C). In contrast, smaller numbers of students will score a B or D. A much smaller percentage of students will score an F or an A. The score grades create a distribution that looks like a bell. The bell curve is symmetrical in that half of the data will fall to the left of the mean, and half will fall to the right.

Eq. (1) is the formula for a normal density function.

$$f(\chi) = \frac{1}{\sqrt{2\pi\sigma}} e^{-(x-\mu)^2/(2\sigma^2)} \, for - \infty < x < +\infty. \tag{1}$$

where $\mu$ and $\sigma$ are the mean and standard deviation of the distribution and are fixed constants. $e^x$ is the exponential function. The mean can take both positive and negative values, including zero, while the standard deviation can only take positive values.

The standard deviation controls the spread of the distribution. If the standard deviation is small, the data will cluster tightly around the mean, and the normal distribution will be taller. A bigger standard deviation indicates more dispersion away from the mean, and the normal distribution will be flatter and wider. Below are the properties of a standard normal distribution.

- The mean, mode and median are all equal.
- The curve is symmetric around the mean, μ.
- Half of the values are to the left of the centre, and exactly half the values are to the right.
- The total area under the curve is 1.

### *2.1.3 Lognormal distribution*

The lognormal distribution is a continuous probability distribution of a random variable whose logarithm is normally distributed [8, 9]. If the random variable $X$ is log-normally distributed, then $Y = ln\,(X)$ has a normal distribution. A random variable which is log-normally distributed takes only positive values. The probability density function for a lognormal distribution is defined by two parameters, namely the mean[1] $\mu$ and the standard deviation $\sigma$:

$$N(\ln(x); \mu, \sigma) = \frac{1}{\sqrt[\sigma]{2\pi}} exp\left[\frac{(\ln(x) - \mu)^2}{2\sigma^2}\right], x > 0 \tag{2}$$

The shape of the lognormal distribution is defined by three parameters:$\sigma$ is the **shape** parameter and is known as the standard deviation for the lognormal distribution. The shape parameter affects the general shape of the distribution and can be

[1] These two parameters should not be mistaken for the mean or standard deviation from a normal distribution. When the data is transformed using natural logarithms, the mean is the mean of the transformed data, and the standard deviation is the standard deviation of the transformed data.

calculated from historical data. The shape parameter does not change the location or height of the graph; it affects the overall shape, while the **location** parameter $\mu$ tells you where on the x-axis the graph is located. The probability density function for a lognormal distribution is defined by two parameters, namely the mean and the standard deviation. Lognormal distributions can model growth rates that frequently occur in biology and financial areas. It also models time to failure in reliability studies. The lognormal distribution is widely used in situations where values are positively skewed, for example, in financial analysis for security valuation or in real estate for property valuation, and where values cannot fall below zero. Stock prices are usually positively skewed rather than normally (symmetrically) distributed. Stock prices exhibit this trend because they cannot fall below the lower limit of zero but might increase to any price without limit. Therefore, the lognormal distribution curve can be used to identify the compound return that the stock can expect to achieve over some time. Similarly, real estate prices illustrate positive skewness and are log-normally distributed as property values cannot become negative.

### *2.1.4 Bernoulli distribution*

A Bernoulli distribution is a discrete probability distribution for a Bernoulli trial — a random experiment that has only two outcomes (a 'Success' or a 'Failure'). The two outcomes are labelled by $n = 0$ and $n = 1$ in which $n = 1$ ('success') occurs with probability $p$ and $n = 0$ ('failure') occurs with probability $q \equiv 1 - p$, where $0 < p < 1$. The probability density function for a Bernoulli distribution is given as:

$$P(n) = \begin{cases} 1 - p & for \quad n = 0 \\ p & for \quad n = 1 \end{cases} \tag{3}$$

The distribution of heads and tails in coin tossing is an example of a Bernoulli distribution with

$$p = q = ½.$$

### *2.1.5 Triangular distribution*

The triangular probability distribution is a continuous distribution that has a probability density function shaped like a triangle. The triangular distribution is defined by three parameters, namely: minimum value (Min), most likely value (Likely) and maximum value (Max). This distribution is practical in real-world applications because we can often estimate the minimum, most likely and maximum value that a random variable will take. So, we can often model the behaviour of random variables by using a triangular distribution with the knowledge of these three values. Essentially, we can use this distribution when we only have limited information about distribution but can estimate the upper and lower bounds, as well as the most likely value. The three conditions underlying the triangular distribution are:

1. The minimum number of items is fixed.

2. The maximum number of items is fixed.

3. The most likely number of items falls between the minimum and maximum values, forming a triangular-shaped distribution.

Values near the minimum and maximum are less likely to occur than those near the most likely value. The equation for the triangular distribution is given below:

$$f(x) = \begin{cases} \dfrac{2(x - Min)}{(Max - Min)(Likely - Min)} \textit{ for } Min < x < Likely \\[2ex] \dfrac{2(Max - x)}{(Max - Min)(Max - Likely)} \textit{ for } Likely < x < Max \end{cases} \tag{4}$$

## 3. Dealing with uncertainty using probabilistic models

Uncertainty in decision analytics emanates from a lack of knowledge about the system being modelled, and it consists of random events or variables. For example, addressing questions such as 'what are the average future demands for our products?' and 'Should we invest in a capital project or not?' The most common type of uncertainty is uncertainty due to randomness. Uncertainty can be qualitative or quantitative. Qualitative uncertainty may be due to a lack of knowledge about the factors that affect demand. In contrast, quantitative uncertainty may come from a lack of precise knowledge of a model parameter or a lack of confidence that the mathematical model is a correct formulation of the problem. Uncertainty can impact our decisions and actions in desirable as well as undesirable ways. Uncertainty can be reduced by collecting more information or data (i.e., quantitative methods). One of the most commonly used quantitative methods to address uncertainty is the probabilistic modelling using the Monte Carlo method.

Most business decisions are based on a forecast of future variables. These variables could be net present value (NPV), net profit, demand for a product, etc. The future is uncertain. To provide a decision-maker with helpful information, you need to generate a comprehensive range of potential outcomes and their relative likelihoods to make the best possible decisions. Our aim in decision analytics is to reduce uncertainty in our business decisions by envisioning possible scenarios and making forecasts based on what is considered probable within a range of probabilities. All probabilistic models have the following in common:

1. Correct probability distributions,

2. Correct use of the input data for these distributions,

3. Accounting for the associations and relationships between variables.

Selecting the correct probability distributions for the input variables is essential to maximize your results' confidence. The uncertain input probability distributions should be as realistic as possible. Remember that each distribution has distinctive ranges of possible sampled values and associated probabilities/likelihoods. Therefore, choosing the wrong distribution will create the wrong simulation data. A natural question at this point would be how do we know the 'right' probability distributions for our variables? Unfortunately, this is a challenging question, a complete discussion of which is beyond the scope of this chapter. However, some guidelines will enable you to create reasonable models. We will provide a brief discussion of each in turn below.

**Discrete or Continuous Data:** Probability distributions describe the dispersion of the values of a random variable. Therefore, the type of a variable determines the type of probability distribution. The distribution for a single random variable is divided into discrete and continuous distributions. When identifying the 'right' probability distribution for your dataset, the first question is to examine whether the variable or quantity is discrete or continuous. A ***discrete*** quantity has a finite or countable number of possible values — for example, the gender of a person or the country of a person's birth. A ***continuous*** quantity can take on any number in the natural number line and has infinitely many possible values within a specified range. An example is the household incomes of Africans living in Scotland. Discrete probability distributions or probability mass functions are used for discrete variables, and probability density functions are used for continuous variables. For discrete probability distribution functions, each possible value has a non-zero likelihood.

**Is the Variable Bounded or Unbounded**? The second way of identifying a probability distribution that fits your dataset is to know if the continuous variable is bounded - that is, does it have a minimum and maximum value? Some continuous variables have exact lower bounds. For example, the price of a stock on a particular trading day cannot be less than zero. Some quantities also have exact upper bounds. For example, the percentage of a population exposed to the SARS-COV-2 virus (COVID-19) cannot be greater than 100%. Most real-world variables have de facto bounds - that is, it is plausible to assert that there is zero probability that the quantity would be smaller than some lower bound or larger than some upper bound, even though there is no precise way to determine the bound.

The discussions so far relate to where you have historical datasets. Historical data is often a reasonable indicator of the distribution of future outcomes for the input variable, both in terms of the general shape and parameter estimates. However, it is important to note that there is always an implicit assumption that the historical data is an 'accurate' representation of the future. But historical data has some possible flaws that need to be considered. For instance, is the data genuinely representative of the potential future, that is, how similar will the future conditions be to those in the past? Second, what is the sample period? - Does the data only go back over a short period. The sample period is vital because certain observations could be over or under-represented?

**Theory and Subject Matter Knowledge**: It is not uncommon to encounter situations in practice where there is no historical data. A suitable process has to be followed to derive reasonable probability distributions and parameters in such circumstances. We consider a method that can be used to choose a probability distribution in the absence of historical data. A mathematical theory or logic will determine the correct distribution in most situations. For instance, a lognormal distribution is commonly used to describe distributions of financial assets such as share prices in the literature. This is because asset prices cannot be negative [10, 11]. Caution must be applied when using theory to choose the proper probability distribution that fits a dataset. There may be assumptions in theory that may not be valid in your situation. Examples include using a Binomial to model the sum of several identical and independent Bernoulli processes.

## 4. Application of probabilistic modelling using Monte Carlo simulation in business decision making

### 4.1 The problem

CEDFA Ltd. deals in new and used cars. The firm has secured a franchise with a major car manufacturer and ordered two car models—saloon and hatchback models. Due to changes in market forces, the unit costs and the demand for the cars are unknown. The firm estimated the demands for each model based on the previous year's data. According to the franchise agreement, any vehicles not sold by the end of the year will need to be discounted to ensure they are sold. The size of the discount is affected by various factors, including the presence of alternative brands in the market. The firm anticipates that the annual franchise fee could increase this year as the contract expires and has estimated the probability of this increase to be 0.25. If it does, the cost will be $5,000,000. Based on the historical data, the firm's sales and market analysts have come up with the base-case estimates shown in **Table 1** below.

| Variable description | Amount (£) |
|---|---|
| Unit cost of a saloon | $18,000 |
| Unit cost of a hatchback | $25,500 |
| Sales price per saloon | $21,000 |
| Sales price per hatchback | $26,000 |
| An increase in franchise fee | $5,000,000 |
| Number of units purchased | |
| Number of saloon cars purchased | 3000 |
| Number of hatchback cars purchased | 2000 |
| Demand for the cars (At full price) | |
| Demand for saloon cars | 2500 |
| Demand for hatchback | 1500 |
| Discount rates for unsold cars | |
| Saloon discount rate | 15% |
| Hatchback | 25% |
| Probability of increasing franchise fee | 0.25 |

**Table 1.**
*Base case estimates.*

The company is worried about how the uncertainty in the business environment would affect the demands for their cars and the subsequent discount rates to be used in discounting the unsold vehicles as per their franchise agreement. Based on the collected data, the company's analysts estimate that the unit cost for each car and the demand for each car follow the *triangular probability distribution* and the discount rates follow the *lognormal probability distribution*. The analysts suggest the *Bernoulli probability distribution* to model the potential increase in the franchise fee. These probability distributions represent the uncertainty in these variables, the full range of

| | Minimum value | Most likely value | Maximum value | |
|---|---|---|---|---|
| Unit cost of saloon | $17,500 | $18,000 | $20,000 | |
| Unit cost of hatchback | $21,500 | $22,500 | $25,000 | |
| Demand for saloon at full price | 1000 | 2500 | 3000 | |
| Demand for a hatchback at full price | 500 | 1500 | 2000 | |
| **Discount rate (Lognormal distribution)** | | | | |
| | **Mean** | **Standard Deviation** | **Trunc Min** | **Trunc Max** |
| Discount to sell leftover saloon | 15% | 7% | 10% | 30% |
| Discount to sell leftover hatchback | 25% | 10% | 15% | 40% |
| Probability of increase in franchise fee | | 0.25 | | |

**Table 2.**
*Probability distribution parameters.*

possibilities and how likely they are. **Table 2** below shows the parameters for the probability distributions.

Given that the company will have to discount any leftover car as per the franchise agreement, the company wants to know the effects of the different discount rates on the net profit. Based on historical experience and the current market environment, the firm anticipates that the minimum discount it can give for unsold saloon and hatchback cars would be 10% and 15%, respectively. At the same time, the maximum discount rate is estimated as 30% and 40%, respectively. As part of the firm's strategic business decisions, the company executives want to understand the impact of the unit costs, the potential increase in the franchise fee, the demand for the cars and the discount rates on the firm's net profit. Also, the firm wants to decide the minimum and maximum discount rates to apply to the unsold cars and the variable with the most significant impact on the total revenue and net profit.

For this example, we are required to do the following:

a. Build a total revenue/net profit model

b. Use the triangular probability distribution to propagate uncertainty in the unit cost and demand for the saloon and hatchback vehicles.

c. Use the lognormal distribution to account for the uncertainty in the discount rate.

d. Perform 50,000 iterations and 2 simulations, and determine the probability of incurring a loss at 95% confidence interval.

e. Perform a sensitivity analysis and determine the variable with the largest effect on net profit. (Contributions to variance).

### 4.2 Decision scenarios

The company wants to decide the discount rate to apply to unsold cars at the end of the year. To make this decision, the firm created two scenarios, namely, *strategy one -*

allowing the discount rate to be as high as possible (untruncated or unbounded), and *strategy two* - truncating (or bounded) the discount rate with minimum and maximum rates, as shown in **Table 2** above. Evaluate the effects of these two different strategies on the firm's net profit.

### 4.3 Solutions

As you can see, most business decisions depend on several different uncertain factors/variables. Suppose we assume that we can determine or estimate the probability distributions of the individual variables. We can then aggregate these into the probability distribution of the output variable. A commonly used approach is Monte Carlo simulation. In the Monte Carlo simulation method, the probability distribution of the output variable is determined by using a large sample of randomly generated values for the individual variables. These values are drawn from the known or estimated probability distributions of the different input variables or directly from corresponding historical data. Monte Carlo simulations do not make distributional assumptions for the individual probability distributions, and correlations between these variables can be easily considered. In Monte Carlo methods, we perform many simulations and iterations. This is because of the principle of the Central Limit Theorem[2].

To account for the uncertainties in the input variables, the company's analysts estimate that the unit cost for each car and the demand for each car follow the triangular probability distribution. The discount rates follow the lognormal probability distribution as shown in **Table 2**. The analysts suggest the Bernoulli probability distribution to model the potential increase in the franchise fee. Furnished with these pieces of information, we start the modelling process.

First, we develop a deterministic model using the base-case estimates of the input variables provided by the firm. A deterministic model is a model that does not account for randomness/uncertainty in the input variables that are used in forecasting the output variable of interest[3] [12]. Consequently, a deterministic model will always produce the same output from a given starting condition. The output from the deterministic model (**Table 3**) assumes that the unit cost, demand and the discount rate applied to sell leftover cars for both the saloon and hatchback models are constant over time. However, we know that these variables are outside the control of the decision-maker and can change over time. For instance, the demand for these cars is not known with certainty. Some of the factors that affect demand could include the presence of substitutes in the market, the business cycle[4] and the advertisement budget, amongst others. So based on a discount rate of 15% and 25% applied to leftover saloon and hatchback, the firm will end up with total revenue of $110,175,000 and a profit of $11,175,000.

---

[2] The central limit theorem posits that the probability distribution of a sum of independent random variables can be approximated by a normal distribution if the number of individual random variables is large enough.

[3] The variables of interest in this example are the total revenue and the profit.

[4] Business cycles are intervals of expansion (economic booms) followed by a recession (burst) in economic activity [13]. Business cycles have implications for the welfare of the wider population and businesses.

| Variables | Calculations |
|---|---|
| Total saloon cost | $54,000.00 |
| Total hatchbacks cost | $45,000.00 |
| Total cost (including franchise fee increase) | $99,000,000.00 |
| Total saloon revenue | $61,425,000.00 |
| Total hatchback revenue | $48,750,000.00 |
| Total revenue | **$110,175,000.00** |
| Profit | **$11,175,000** |

**Table 3.**
*Total revenue and profit: deterministic model.*

It is easy to observe the challenges of relying on this model to make business decisions:

1. This model does not consider the variabilities or uncertainties in the input variables.

2. While we can see the potential net profit, we cannot determine the probability of ending up with this amount at the end of the period.

3. This model does not allow us to envision or see the possible values the net profit can take, alongside the probabilities of taking on those values.

Why is this important? This is important because we may be able to evaluate the potential downside risk of our decision. That is the probability of making a loss.

We will illustrate how to use probability distributions to propagate uncertainty in the input variables. We use Monte Carlo simulation to produce information and insights from our model and its assumptions. As alluded to in the previous section, the precision of a probabilistic model relies heavily on the appropriate use of probability distributions to accurately represent the problem's uncertainty, randomness and variability. In practice, inappropriate use of probability distributions is a common failure of probabilistic models. We start by replacing the 'fixed' estimates of the input variables in the model in table three with the parameters for the probability distributions in table two. Second, we will mark the variables of interest (total revenue and net profit) as the 'output' cells. These two variables are the variables we want to analyze. The simulation[5] exercise allows us to sample all the input distributions randomly and recalculates the spreadsheet repeatedly, keeping track of the resulting output values. Each separate recalculation in the simulation process is known as an 'iteration'. A single iteration represents a possible future set of circumstances in the model. So, two iterations represent two possible future sets of circumstances in the model. Since the sampling is random, commonly occurring input ranges and combinations of inputs would appear more frequently in the simulation data. On the other hand, rarer scenarios will be less likely. We present the output from the probabilistic Monte Carlo simulation models for the two strategies. The probability density graphs with some statistics are reported in **Figures 1** and 2.

[5] We used the Palisade @Risk software for the probabilistic modeling.

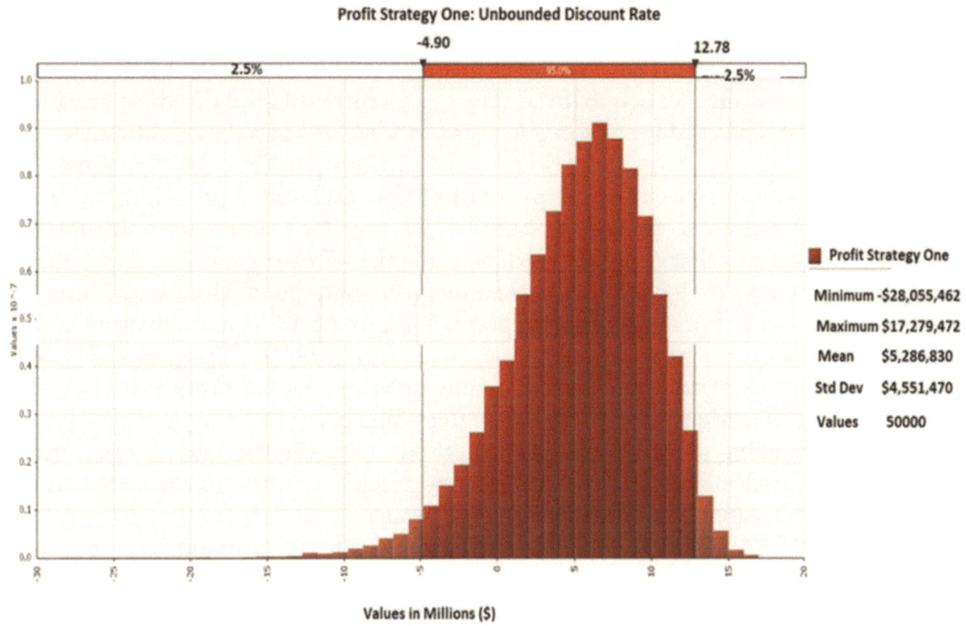


**Figure 1.**
*Profit strategy one (Untruncated Discount Rates).*

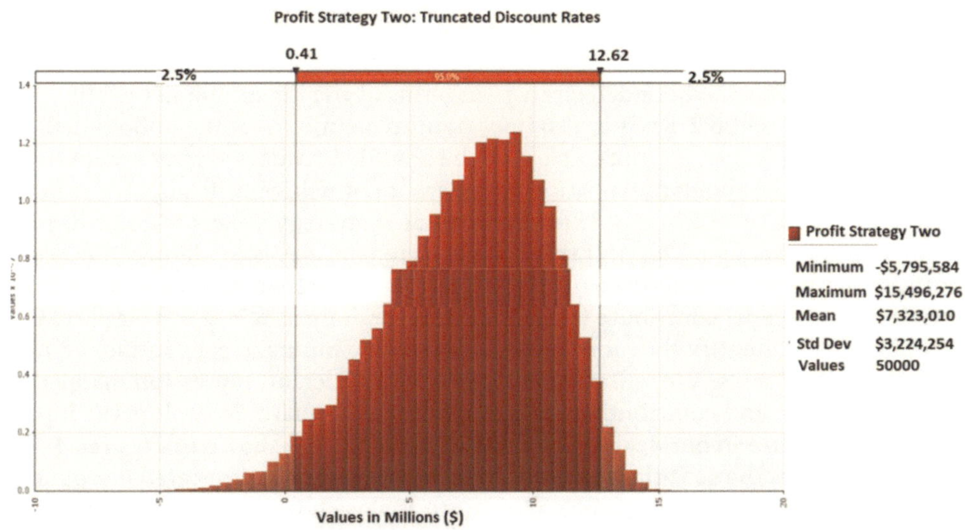


**Figure 2.**
*Profit strategy two (Truncated Discount Rates).*

The primary purpose of quantifying uncertainties is to obtain a sound basis for our decisions. As you can see, all available information on an uncertain (random) variable is, in principle, contained in the corresponding probability distributions (see **Figures 1** and **2**). In decision analytics, a well-informed decision is based on comparing the decision-maker's risk appetite or risk tolerance threshold to the outcomes they are exposed to. For instance, we may be interested in evaluating the probability of incurring a loss or reaching a defined target. The outputs from our model allow us to achieve these goals. Statistics such as the mean or standard deviation of the output variable are also computed. These statistics are used to describe various future outcomes. For **strategy one**, we see that the effect of an **untruncated** discount rate on the company's bottom line could result in a loss of ($4,900,126) at a 95% confidence interval. The probability of realizing this loss for this company is 2.5%. The same strategy could result in a potential net profit of $12,780,912 with a probability of 97.5%.

We turn our attention to the second scenario, **strategy two**, where we **truncate/limit** the amount of discount that could be used in selling the leftover cars. The idea is that no matter how many cars are left unsold; we cannot go beyond the maximum discount rates for the cars. From the probability density graph in **Figure 2**, we can see that the upper and lower bounds for the net profit are $414,780 and $12,623,794. The probability of ending up with a lower profit is 2.5% and ending up with a higher profit is 97.5%.

Let us briefly consider how we can make decisions using the results from our probabilistic modelling using Monte Carlo methods. Observe the statistics reported in **Figures 1** (truncated model) and **2** (untruncated model). For the untruncated strategy, the highest possible loss that the firm can incur is (£28,055,462), and the maximum profit is £17,279,472. While for the truncated strategy, the maximum loss is (£5,795,584), and the maximum potential profit is £15,496,276. Although the firm may earn a slightly higher profit if they allow market forces to determine how much discount they can apply to unsold cars, it is clear from the reported statistics that this strategy is riskier than the bounded discount rate strategy. **Table 4** shows a comparison of the two strategies.

Observe from **Table 4** that the bounded/truncated strategy outperforms the untruncated strategy in key metrics like maximum loss ($5,795,584, vs. $28,055,462) and expected profit ($7,323,010 vs. $5,286,830). On the other hand, the unbounded strategy outperforms the bounded strategy in terms of the maximum net profit ($17,279,472 vs. $15,496,276). It is also important to mention that the unbounded/untruncated strategy carries more risk than the bounded/truncated strategy. In this example, we use the standard deviation as a measure of risk. Specifically, we see a standard deviation of $3,224,254.35 for the truncated strategy versus $4,551,470 for the untruncated strategy. The next thing we need to consider is to identify our key inputs using sensitivity analysis. Sensitivity analyses study how various sources of uncertainty in a model contribute to the model's overall uncertainty or volatility. Our primary goal is to identify the most 'critical' inputs, the inputs to concentrate on most when making decisions. We will use the regression coefficient, regression mapped values, correlation and contributions to variance tornado charts to explore the inputs we need to prioritize in our decision-making. The results are shown in **Figures 3–6**.

We will discuss the sensitivity graphs from strategy one (untruncated discount rate) for brevity. The tornado graphs allow us to analyse how the inputs in our

| Comparison metrics | Untruncated strategy | Truncated strategy |
|---|---|---|
| Maximum net loss | −$28,055,462 | −$5,795,584 |
| Maximum net profit | $17,279,472 | $15,496,276 |
| Expected profit | $5,286,830 | $7,323,010 |
| Standard deviation | $4,551,470 | $3,224,254 |

**Table 4.**
*Comparison of the two Strategies (unbounded and Bounded Strategies).*

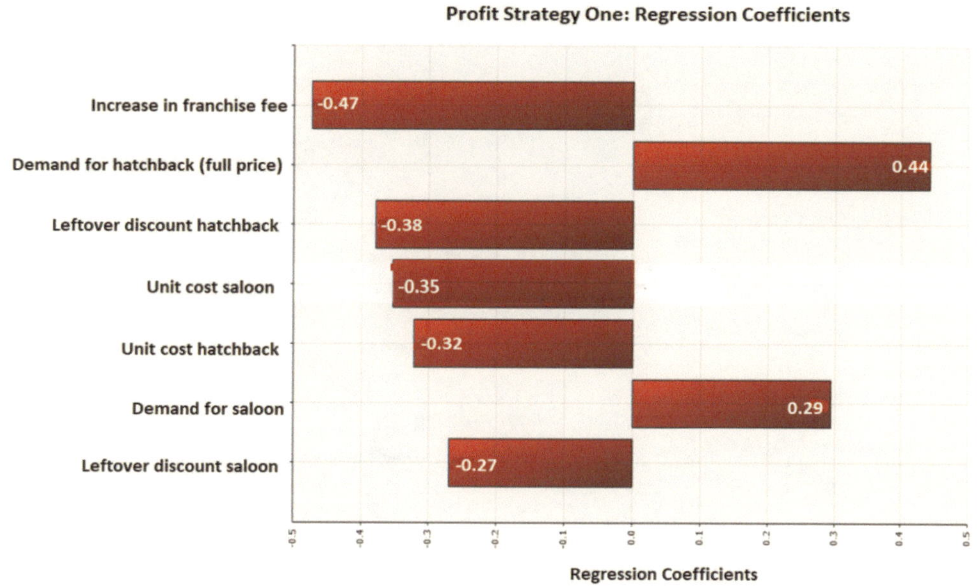


**Figure 3.**
*Sensitivity tornado graph (Estimated Regression Coefficient).*

decision model drive the variations/behaviour of our output variables (in this case, the net profit). Variables with the most considerable impact on the output distribution have the longest bars in the graph.

Looking at the regression coefficients (**Figure 3**), we see that increase in the franchise fee has the biggest impact on the net profit. Specifically, if the franchise fee is increased by 1%, that increase will result in a 0.47% decrease in the net profit. The demand for the hatchback model is another variable with a great impact on the net profit. If the demand increases by 1%, this will result in a 0.44% increase in the net profit, while a similar increase in the demand for the saloon model will result in a 0.29% increase in profit[6]. Also, increasing the discount rates for both hatchback and saloon models by one per cent would result in a reduction in net profit of 0.38% and 0.27%, respectively. The company should also pay attention to the unit costs of both models. Specifically, a one per cent increase in the unit cost of saloon and hatchback cars will result in 0.35% and 0.32%, respectively.

In monetary terms, the firm may lose up to $2,163,404.38 for a 1% increase in the franchise fee while holding all the other variables constant - see **Figure 4** below. Similarly, an increase in the demand for the hatchback model will lead to about a $2,023,527.94 increase in the net profit. In addition, increasing the discount rates will result in a reduction in profit. For the hatchback cars, increasing the discount rate by 1% will lead to about $1,736,223.46 loss in profit; a similar increase in the discount rate for the saloon cars will lead to a $1,226,373.03 loss in profit. Based on these pieces of information, the firm can make an informed decision while taking its risk appetite and equity capital into consideration.

[6] The key to interpreting the graphs is to consider both the signs (positive or negative) and the magnitude of the estimated coefficients.

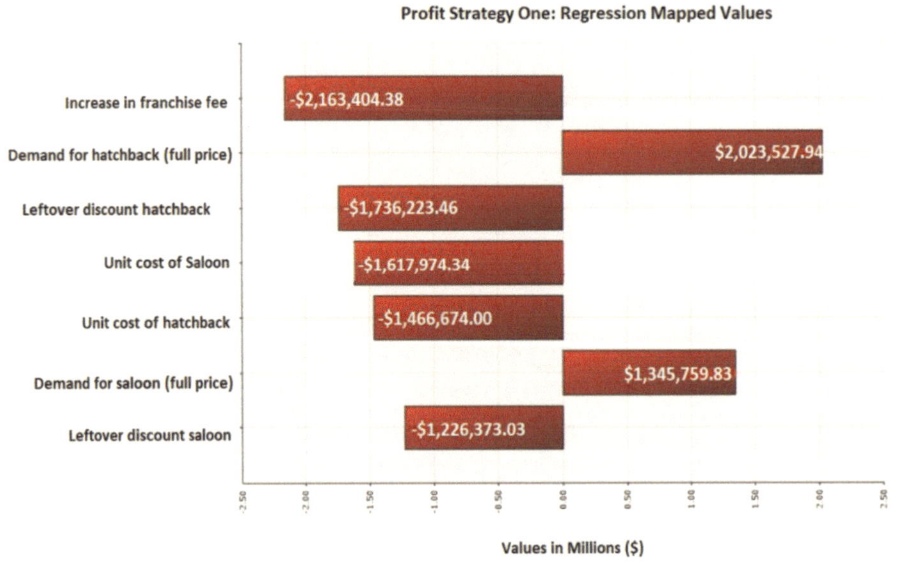


**Figure 4.**
*Regression mapped values.*

Understanding the interdependency of the input variables in the model is very important. Correlation measures the extent to which two variables vary together, including the strength and direction of their relationship. Exploring the correlation between variables is an essential part of exploratory data analysis. A high correlation indicates a strong relationship, and a weak correlation indicates that they are not closely related. **Figure 5** reveals a negative correlation between the increase in franchise fee, unit cost and discount rate and a positive correlation between demand and net profit.

We look at the contribution to the variance tornado graph (**Figure 6**) below. This graph allows us to explore the contributions of each of the input variables to changes in the output variable. Again, we see that changes in the franchise fee cause 22.7% of

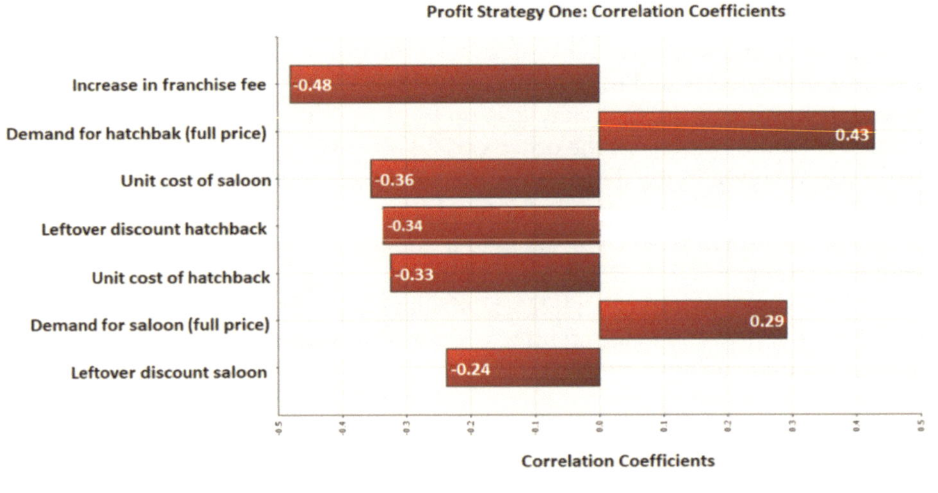


**Figure 5.**
*Correlation analysis.*

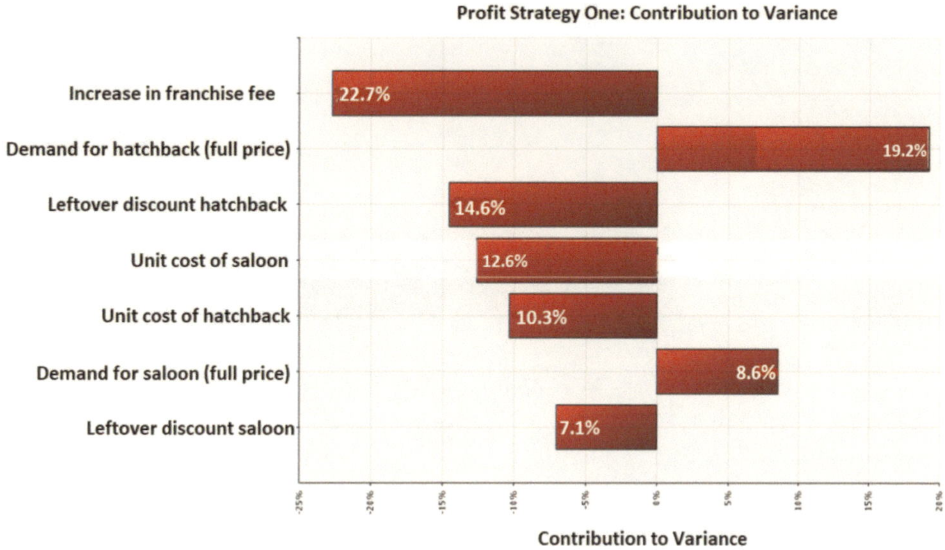


**Figure 6.**
*Contribution to variance.*

the variation in the output variable, while the demand for hatchback cars caused 19.2% amongst others.

Finally, we look at scenario analysis. We are particularly interested in examining a combination of input variables that contribute significantly towards reaching a specific goal, also referred to as the **target scenario** associated with the output values. In this case, we want to examine the combination of input variables that could result in the following:

1. Achieve a net profit value over the 75th percentile, i.e., $8,624,840.69 75th percentile in the probability density.

2. A second scenario is a net loss or no profit. That is a worst-case scenario.

3. The final scenario achieves a net profit over the 90th percentile, $10,777,718.05 (90th percentile in the probability density).

The results from the three scenarios analysis are reported in **Figures 7–9** below.

Our first desired scenario is to explore the possibility of having a net profit in the 75th percentile[7]. In the net profit probability distribution, we locate the 75th percentile as $8,624,840.69. The scenario analysis identifies the input combinations that have the most significant effect in achieving this net profit. Looking at **Figure 7** above, we can see that the strategy that would allow the firm to achieve the desired scenario is to increase the demand for hatchback cars at full price by 0.54% and reduce the unit cost of saloon cars to 0.50%. Essentially, scenario analysis helps you identify the input combinations that have the most significant effect in achieving a net profit value at

[7] Percentiles indicate the percentage of values that fall below a particular value. They tell you where a value stands relative to other values. The general rule is that if value *Y* is at the Nth percentile, then *Y* is greater than *N*% of the values.

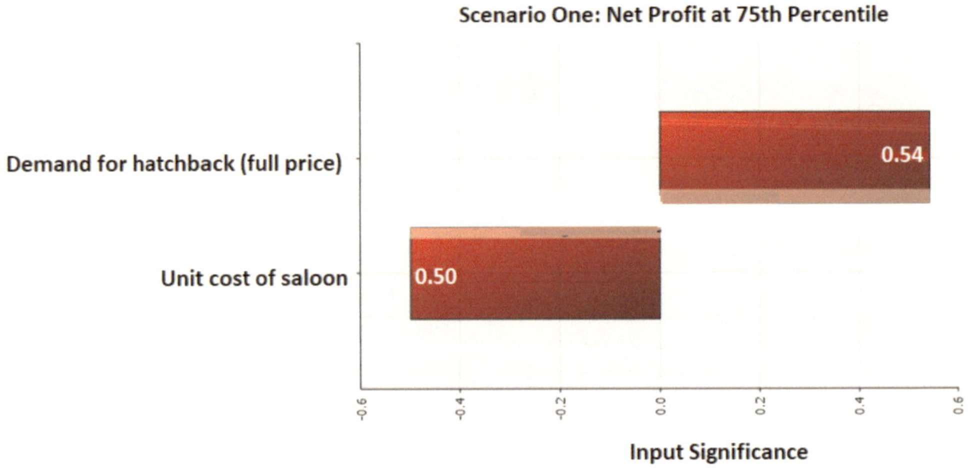


**Figure 7.**
*Net profit at the 75th percentile.*

the 75th percentile. Given that the unit cost of the saloon cars is outside the firm's control, the company may try and negotiate a discount with the manufacturer by increasing the number of vehicles ordered.

**Figure 8** below provides the second scenario, which is the worst-case scenario. Observe that increasing the franchise fee by 2.3%, a drop in demand for the hatchback of 0.66%, and an increase in the discount rate applied to leftover hatchbacks will result in a loss. We are always concerned with the worst-case scenario in risk and decision analytics. At this stage, the firm needs to decide whether to continue with this franchise or look for alternative manufacturers. Nevertheless, they must block any attempt to increase the franchise fee by more than 2%.

The final scenario shown in **Figure 9** below, which is the best, achieves a net profit value in the 90th percentile. To achieve the desired target, the firm will have to

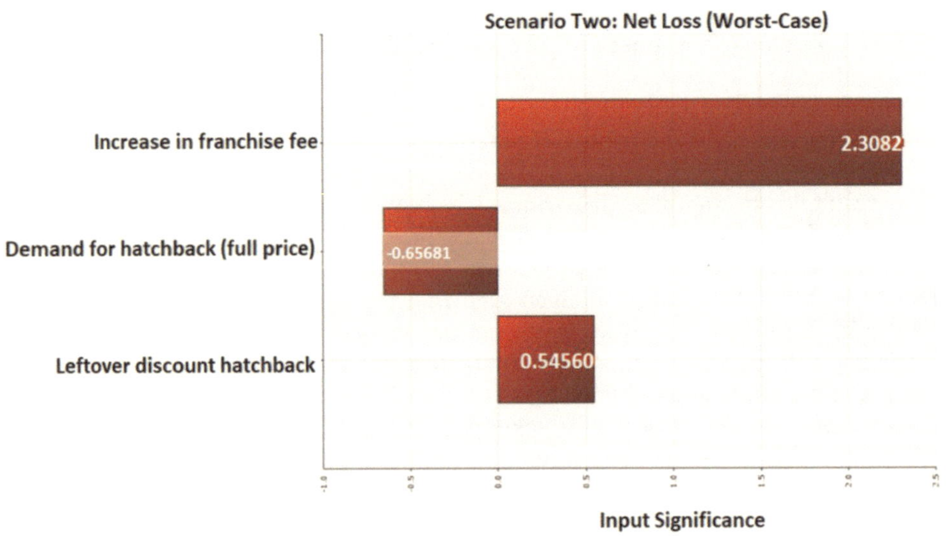


**Figure 8.**
*Net loss (Worst-Case Scenario).*

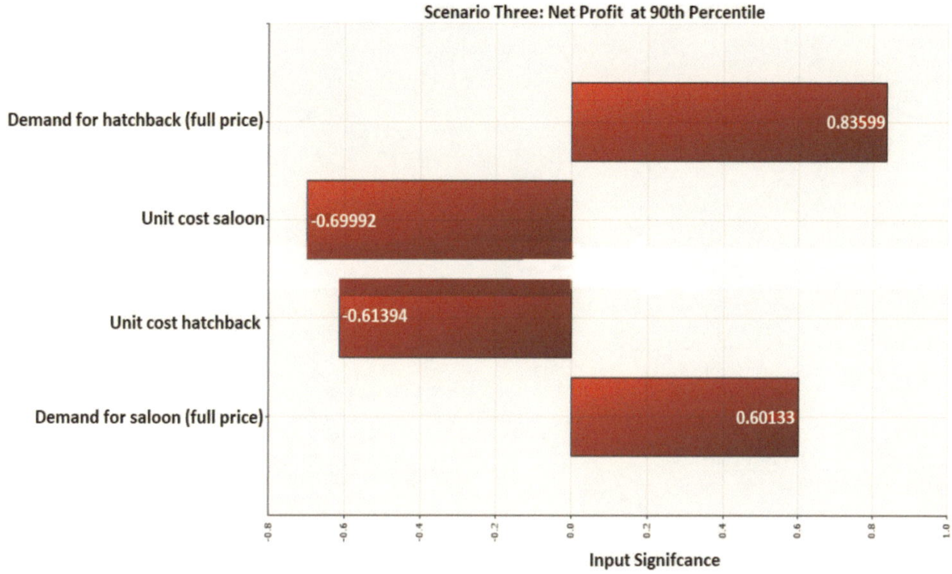


**Figure 9.**
*Net profit at the 90th percentile.*

increase the demand for hatchbacks and saloons by 0.85% and 0.60%, respectively. At the same time, negotiating discounts for the saloons and hatchbacks by 0.70% and 0.60%, respectively. Using probabilistic Monte Carlo methods as an exploratory decision-making tool can improve the decision maker's understanding of the significant business value drivers. This method allows us to appreciate the most relevant uncertain input variables and their sensitivities to the variable of interest. As you can see, much of the value in probabilistic modelling comes from its role in structuring a more constructive management discussion.

## 5. Conclusion

This chapter presents an application of probabilistic modelling using Monte Carlo simulation methods for strategic business decisions. We examined two decision strategies and evaluated the effects of the critical uncertain input variables on the outcome variables. What is apparent from the discussion is that making big strategic business decisions from the 'gut' or using deterministic models could be problematic. This is because deterministic models do not allow us to envision all possible scenarios that could affect our decisions and account for uncertainties in our business decisions. However, the expectation that the likelihood of all possible outcomes in a complex dynamic business problem can be accurately estimated using probabilistic models is unrealistic. Instead, probabilistic modelling using the Monte Carlo simulation method helps to combine all available insights about the relevant uncertainties and their impact on the variable of interest. Probabilistic modelling offers essential support to making risk-informed decisions if used appropriately.

## Author details

Chioma Ngozi Nwafor
Glasgow Caledonian University, Glasgow, Scotland, UK

*Address all correspondence to: chioma.nwafor@gcu.ac.uk

## References

[1] Alon N, Spencer JH. The Probabilistic Method. 2nd ed. New York: Wiley-Interscience; 2000 ISBN 0-471-37046-0

[2] Billingsley P. Probability and Measure. Third ed. New York: Wiley; 1995

[3] Florescu I. Probability and Stochastic Processes. John Wiley & Sons; 2014

[4] Xue J, Zartarian VG, Özkaynak H, Dang W, Glen G, Smith L, et al. A probabilistic exposure assessment for children who contact chromated copper arsenate (CCA)-Treated playsets and decks, Part 2: Sensitivity and uncertainty analyses. Risk Analysis. 2006;**26**:533-541

[5] Sin G, Espuña A. Editorial: Applications of Monte Carlo method in chemical, biochemical and environmental engineering. Frontiers in Energy Research. 2020;**8**:68. DOI: 10.3389/fenrg.2020.00068

[6] Johansen AM. International Encyclopedia of Education. Third ed2010

[7] Keyun Ruan, in Digital Asset Valuation and Cyber Risk Measurement, 2019, Pg. 75-86. doi:10.1016/B978-0-12-812158-0.00004-1

[8] Aitchison J, Brown JAC. The Log normal Distribution, with Special Refere nce to Its Use in Economics. New York: Cambridge University Press; 1957

[9] Crow EL, Shimizu K, editors. Limpert et al. Log-normal Distributions across the Sciences: Keys and Clues. In: Lognormal Distributions: Theory and Applications. New York: Dekker; 1988

[10] Rubinstein M. Implied Binomial Trees. Journal of Finance. 1994;**49**(3): 771-818

[11] Rosenkrantz. Why Stock Prices Have a Lognormal Distribution. University of Manchester at Amherst. Available from: http://janroman.dhis.org/finance/General/log_normal_notes.pdf; 2003. [Accessed: 20 May 2022]

[12] Artzrouni M. Mathematical Demography. Encyclopaedia of Social Measurement2005. pp. 641-651

[13] Harvey AC, Trimbur TM. General model based filters for extracting trends and cycles in economic time series (PDF). Review of Economics and Statistics. 2003;**85**(2):244-255. DOI: 10.1162/003465303765299774. S2CID 57567527

Chapter 4

# Deep Network Model and Regression Analysis Using OLS Method for Predicting Lung Vital Capacity

*Harun Sümbül*

## Abstract

With the advancement of technology, many new devices and methods with machine learning and artificial intelligence (ML-AI) have been developed and these methods have begun to play an important role in human life. ML-AI technology is now widely used in many applications such as security, military, communications, bioengineering, medical treatment, food industry, and robotics. In this chapter, deep learning methods and medical usage techniques that have become popular in recent years will be discussed. Experimental and simulation results and a comprehensive example of the biomedical use of the deep network model will be presented. In addition, the regression analysis using the ordinary least squares (OLS) method for estimating lung vital capacity (VC) will be discussed. The simulation results showed that the VC parameter was predicted with higher than 90% accuracy using the proposed deep network model with real data.

**Keywords:** deep network, data analytics, modeling, simulation, vital capacity, MLPFFNN, artificial intelligent, OLS, regression, spirometer

## 1. Introduction

Due to the new coronavirus disease (COVID-19) epidemic, which has recently spread all over the world and has been declared as a global pandemic by WHO (World Health Organization), many people have been adversely affected. The COVID-19 outbreak damages many organs, especially the lungs, and this poses an extra-large risk for major diseases such as chronic obstructive pulmonary disease (COPD).

COPD is a common public disease known worldwide, and its lethal power is increasing day by day [1]. COPD disease is closely related to lung volumes and capacities [2, 3]. Vital capacity (VC) is one of the most important lung parameters [4]. VC is the maximum volume of air taken into and out of the lungs during breathing [5]. The correct measurement of VC is of greatest importance to provide insights on the diagnostic about lung-related obstructive, restrictive, or mixed diseases. Moreover, knowledge of lung volume changes is very important to track the history of many restrictive and obstructive lung problems and their response to various treatments [6].

VC measurements are used for monitoring diseases [7]. For example, chronic reduction in VC may reduce lung compliance. These physiological changes increase the load on the emaciated respiratory muscles and eventually cause a vicious circle of respiratory dysfunction [8]. The VC value is also related to the disease in amyotrophic lateral sclerosis (ALS) and can provide information about the level of the disease [9]. Measurements of VC are used to predict disease progression and to help identify diaphragm dysfunction (DD) [10]. VC is also a very important parameter used for mechanical noninvasive ventilation [11].

A healthy adult's VC ranges from approximately 3000 to 5000 ml liters [12]. The parameters that affect a person's VC can be listed as age, gender, height, mass, and ethnicity, respectively [13]. Many studies in the literature have been done to measure and predict VC [14]. Lung capacity estimates are also made on radiographic images [15]. But spirometer is the most used device to measure VC [16]. The spirometer is the most commonly used device for collecting information about lung-related diseases [17].

**Figure 1** shows the lung volume and capacity parameters measured with the aid of a spirometer [18].

Although the spirometer is currently the most commonly used measurement tool to measure lung parameters, many of them are not portable (the prices of portable ones are very high), their use requires a technician, it cannot be used in the home environment, since the printouts are on paper instead of recording in digital media, and has a high cost.

Machine learning (ML) algorithms such as artificial intelligence (AI), fuzzy logic (FL) are widely used techniques in biomedical studies. Particularly, deep learning (DL) models, due to their superior performance in prediction and classification problems, have become quite popular recently [19]. As a result of the extensive literature search, a VC prediction study with a deep network structure has not been encountered. In this chapter, unlike the literature, the VC parameter value was successfully estimated using the person's age, height, and weight information using the deep learning technique. This value was measured on real patients using a medical spirometer.

The objective of this chapter is twofold, namely, to:

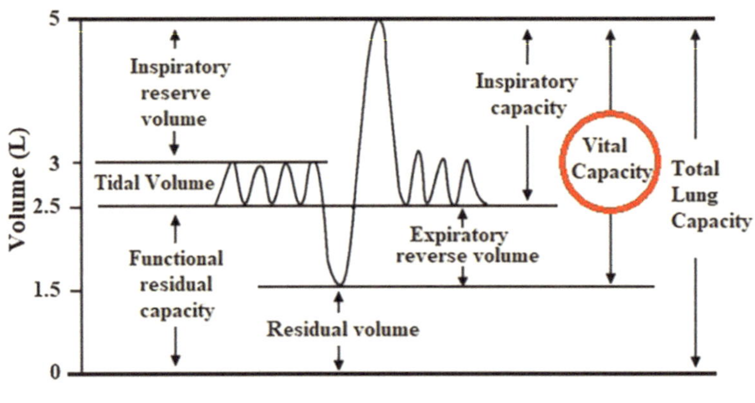


**Figure 1.**
*Lung volume and capacity parameters.*

a. Develop a deep model algorithm that can predict the VC parameter without the need for the spirometer,

b. Understand and measure the effect of input variables on VC from the developed model using OLS regression methods.

## 2. Materials and methods

### 2.1 Spirometric measurements and dataset

The performance success of the DL architecture is closely related to the dataset chosen as its input. The success of DL architectures trained with a large number of data is higher than those with a smaller volume of data. It is known that this type of DL architecture gives positive results in models with sufficient examples but not very deep architecture.

In this book chapter, we collected a biomedical dataset, including VC, age, height, and weight parameters of normal subjects. About 491 healthy subjects (363 males and 128 females, aged between 21 and 61) were selected for this data collection. To measure the VC parameter, the breathing performance of the 50 s was recorded from each patient. Thus, a data record of 6.82 h was created in the database. The measurements were performed using a biomedical spirometer device (Fukuda Sangyo brand spiroanalyz ST-75) at our Biomedical Device Technology Laboratory (BCT Lab). Related information about the patients in the study group is summarized in **Table 1**.

The spirometric measurement system and the device used are shown in **Figure 2**.

At the end of the measurements, a new biomedical dataset consisting of a total of 1.964 data including age, height, and weight, and VC parameters were created. Thus, a data frame with a total of 1.964 data (with a total of 4 columns, each column consisting of 491 values) was created. **Figure 3** shows some sample breathing performance signals of the present dataset.

| Patient No. | Height (cm) | Weight (kg) | Gender (F/M) | BMI (kg/m2) | Age | VC (L) |
|---|---|---|---|---|---|---|
| 1 | 161 | 86 | M | 33.18 | 34 | 6.2 |
| 2 | 166 | 78 | M | 28.31 | 28 | 6.3 |
| 3 | 174 | 91 | M | 30.06 | 32 | 7.7 |
| 4 | 173 | 86 | F | 28.73 | 28 | 5.8 |
| 5 | 166 | 74 | F | 26.85 | 23 | 6.4 |
| 6 | 170 | 93 | M | 32.18 | 24 | 6.9 |
| 7 | 179 | 91 | M | 28.4 | 31 | 7.8 |
| . | . | . | . | . | . | . |
| . | . | . | . | . | . | . |
| . | . | . | . | . | . | . |
| 491 | 169 | 79 | F | 27.66 | 29 | 6.8 |

**Table 1.**
*General features of chosen patients.*

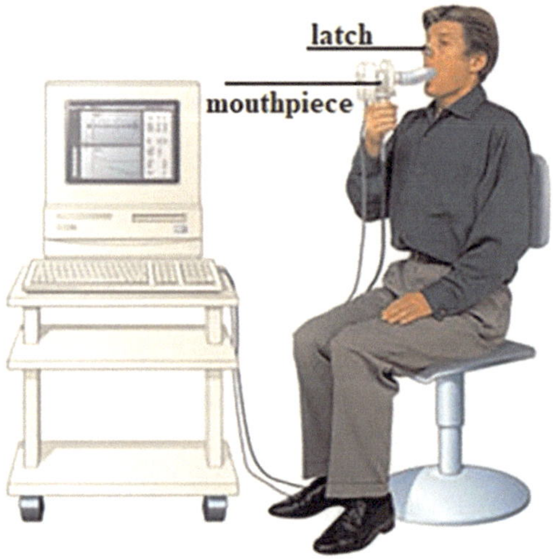


**Figure 2.**
*The spirometric measurement system.*

## 2.2 Proposed deep network model

Neural networks that have more than one hidden layer are called deep neural networks [20]. Deep networks mean that there are multiple hidden layers within the adaptive neural network (ANN) architecture. ANN algorithms can be adapted to many areas and are widely used in many different fields [21]. ANN structurally consists of three layers (input, hidden, and output layer). Neurons between layers are linked to each other by specific pathways that have a certain weight value [22]. In this chapter, as the ANN algorithm, a multilayer perceptron feed-forward neural network (MLPFFNN) was preferred [23]. In MLPFFNN model, data flow occurs in one direction from the input layer to the output layer [24]. The article aims to create a reliable deep model for predicting VC. Weight, height, and age parameters (independent variables) were given as input parameters to the model. The VC value (dependent variable) was taken as output.

The designed MLPFFNN is multilayer and there are many neurons in each layer except the output layer. The number of neurons in the output layer is 1. The number of neurons in the hidden layers was observed gradually between 1 and 70 and by trial and error, and the most ideal multi-neuron network structure was selected. The best result was achieved in 1000 repetitions (the number of repetitions was increased by 50 steps). In the intended deep network model, the mini-batch size is 40. The effect of the mini-batch size on the model performance was examined and after various trials, it was decided that this number was the most ideal. The learning rate was chosen as 0.0012 and gradient reduction as 0.85. Adaptive Moment Estimation (Adam) algorithm is used as the optimizer. The Rectifier Linear Unit (ReLU), which is one of the most commonly used activation functions, is used as an activation function [25], and it is defined as follows:

$$f(x) = \max\{0, x\} \tag{1}$$

where x is the weighted sum of the inputs and f (x) is the activation function. The function output is between 0 and the maximum value. The designed MLPFFNN

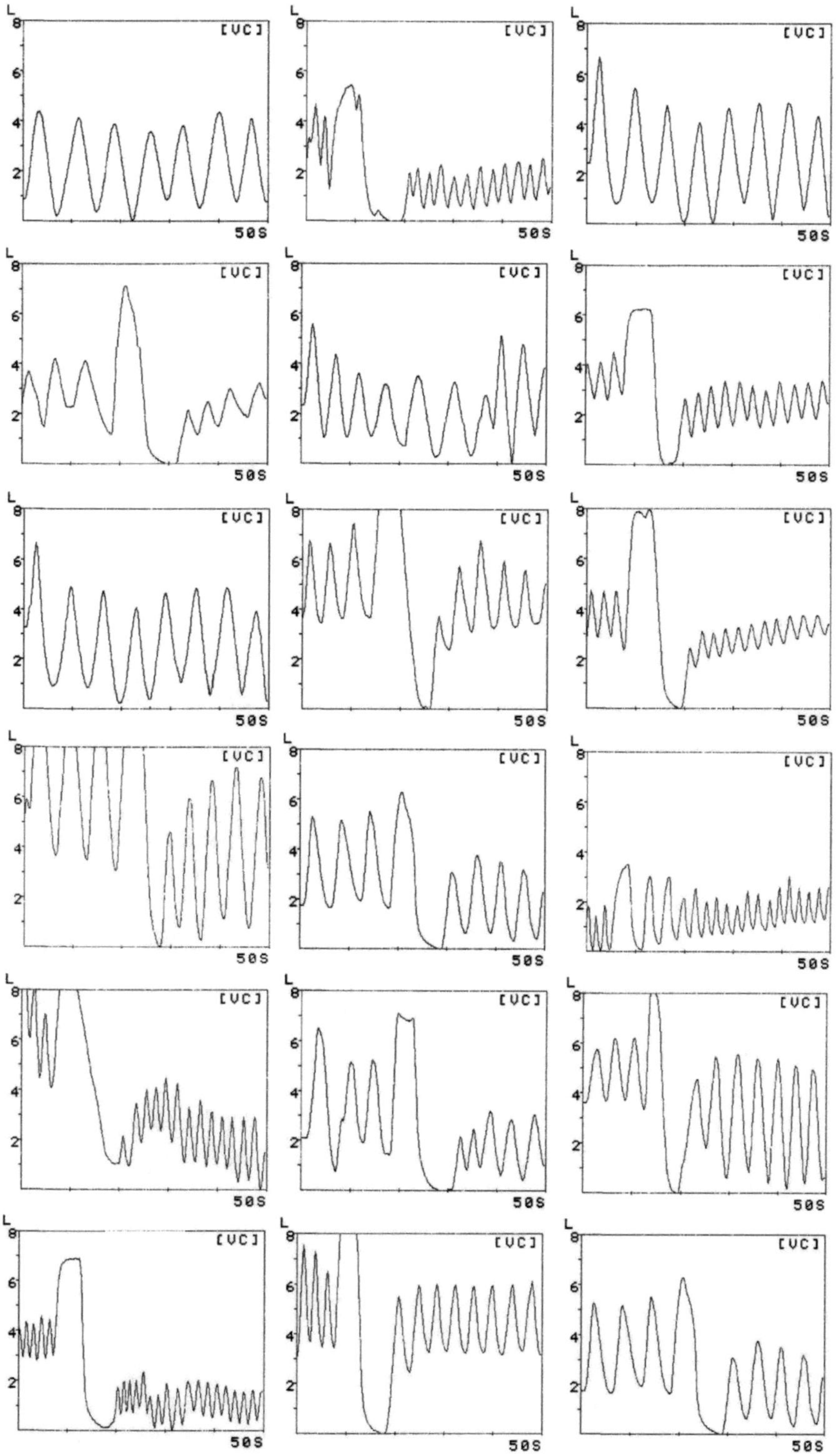

**Figure 3.**
*Sample VC signals from the subject dataset used in this study.*

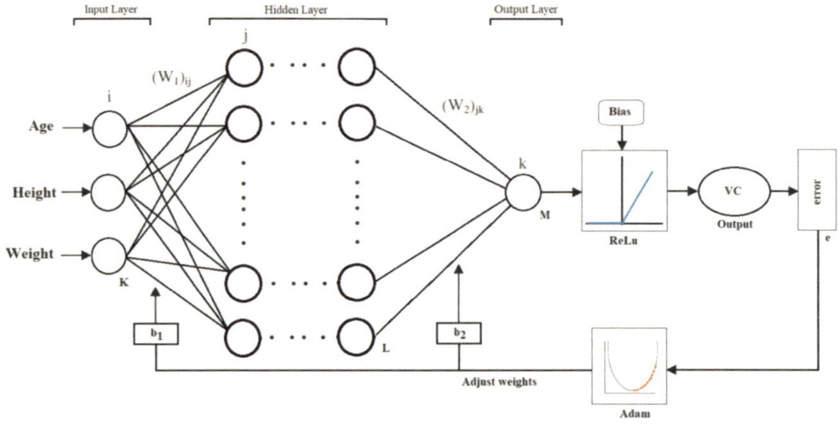


**Figure 4.**
*MLPFFNN architecture.*

structure is shown in **Figure 4**.where, i, j, and k are layers within the model, b1, b2; biases, $w_1$, $w_2$; weights, K, L, M; the number of neurons in the layers, VC; vital capacity.

## 2.3 Training of the proposed MLPFFNN model

In this section, the hyperparameter parameters including learning rate, verbose, batch size, the number of iterations, and epoch size are determined. Adam's optimization algorithm was selected for backpropagation and updating of model weights. To avoid overfitting, the number of epochs was adjusted. Thanks to the dropout feature added to the model, overfitting was prevented. In the drop layer, some nodes of the network are removed to prevent the network from being dependent on a particular neuron. Thanks to "letting go," the network can be forced to learn correctly even in the absence of certain information [26]. The learning rate was reduced gradually. The model algorithm was trained and tested using the 66–33% training and a testing data partition as 329 data, 162 data, respectively. Performance metrics of the proposed model are shown in **Figure 5**. Here, we can see the variation of validation loss (val_loss) compared to training loss (loss). The loss shows how close the neural network is to the optimum. One of the differences between val_loss and loss is that, when using dropout, validation loss can be lower than training loss (usually not expected in cases where dropout is not used). The values for loss are similar. The general loss decreases after almost every epoch and approaches the value 0, whereas the val_loss stagnates.

## 2.4 Regression algorithms

Regression algorithms estimate the output parameter based on the input parameters. OLS is a type of least-squares method used to predict undefined states in a regression model. In the OLS method, in light of the least-squares principle, the sum of the squares of the differences between the dependent variable and the predicted in the given data set is minimized. The differences obtained are aimed to be minimal.

In the OLS model used in the study, the relevance between the dependent variable (VC) and the independent variables (age, height, and weight) was investigated using equation Eq. (2).

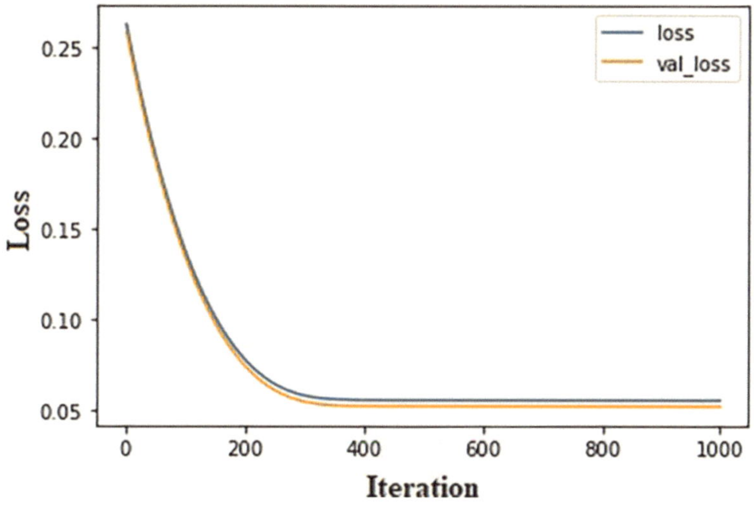


**Figure 5.**
*Training and verification graphs with loss of the model depending on the number of epochs.*

$$A = \alpha_0 + \alpha_1 X_1 + \alpha_2 X_2 + \alpha_3 X_3 + e \tag{2}$$

where A is VC; X1 ... X3 symbolized age, height, and weight variables, respectively; α0 is the bias and α1 ... α3 are the coefficients of the variables; and e is the error parameter [27]. In this study, the relationship between the real values (measured) and the predicted values found by the model was examined by some popular regression methods based on the OLS algorithm.

### *2.4.1 Multi-linear regression (MLR)*

MLR is a statistics-based analysis technique that is widely used in output variable estimation using different variables. The purpose of MLR is to model the linear relationship between the independent variables and the dependent variable.

### *2.4.2 Polynomial regression (PR)*

PR model parameters (X, Y, b, and e) can represent in matrix form, as design input matrix, output response vector, dependent parameters vector, and random error, respectively, as given in Eq. (3) [28].

$$Y = b_0 + b_1 X + b_2 Y + b_3 X_2 + b_4 XY + b_5 Y_2 + e \tag{3}$$

### *2.4.3 Support vector regression (SVR)*

It is known that the SVR algorithm is a very powerful instrument in real value estimation studies [29]. General SVR estimation functions as given in Eq. (4).

$$f(x) = w.\Phi(x) + b \tag{4}$$

where w and b are the weight coefficient and the bias coefficient, respectively [30].

#### *2.4.4 Decision tree regression (DTR)*

DTR is a supervised learning method used for classification and regression. The decision tree-based regression algorithm can provide close to optimum distribution decisions [31].

#### *2.4.5 Random forest regression (RFR)*

RFR is a group learning algorithm based on decision trees. Random forests for regression are formed by growing trees depending on a random vector [32]. The output values are numerical and it is assumed that the training set is independently drawn from the distribution of the random vector Y, X. h (x) and E represents the tree predictor and the mean-squared generalization error for any numerical predictor, respectively. The mean-squared generalization error h(x) is given in Eq. (5).

$$E_{X,Y}\ (Y - h(X))^2 \tag{5}$$

In regression tasks, the mean prediction of K regression trees, $h_k(x)$ is calculated to obtain the random forest prediction is given in Eq. (6).;

$$\text{RFR prediction} = \frac{1}{K}\sum_{k=1}^{K}(h_k(x)) \tag{6}$$

### 2.5 Model Performance Evaluation

To evaluate our proposed method, accuracy is calculated using Eq. (7).

$$\text{Accuracy} = \frac{TP + TN}{TP + TN + FP + FN} \tag{7}$$

TP, TN, FP, and FN in Eq. (6) are true positives, true negatives, false positives, and false negatives, respectively [33]. A confusion matrix has been formed for calculating the performances of the model used in the study.

## 3. Results

In this book chapter, the multiple-layer perceptron neural network (MLPFFNN) was selected for the ANN implementation. In the selected MLPFFNN design, the best result was achieved in 1000 repetitions (the number of repetitions was increased by 50 steps) with a mini-batch size of 40, a learning ratio of 0.0012, and the gradient reduction of 0.85. The simulation environment is Python 3.8.5(64 bit). **Figure 6** shows the predictive VC values found by the model versus the actual VC values.

Statistically, the actual value is the value that is obtained by observation or by measuring the available data. The predicted value is the value of the variable predicted based on the regression analysis.

As a result of the graphical comparison, it can be easily seen that the estimated VC values of all the participants participating in the study watch very close to the actually measured (with spirometer) VC values.

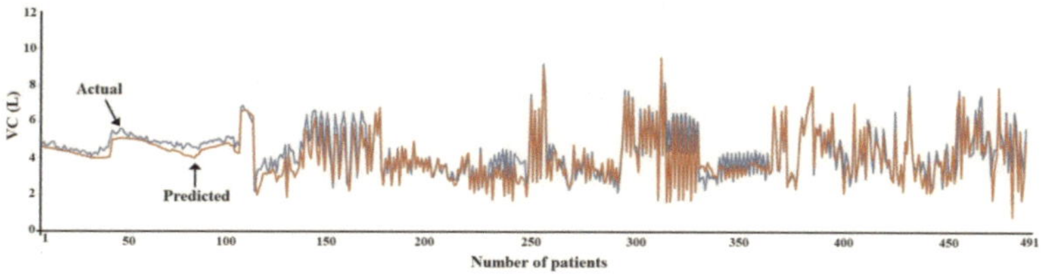


**Figure 6.**
*The graphical comparison of results.*

| R-squared | MLR | PR | SVR | DTR | RFR |
|---|---|---|---|---|---|
| | 0.948 | 0.794 | 0.874 | 0.775 | 0.889 |

**Table 2.**
*Three-parameter OLS models result in terms of R-squared.*

When 3-parameter OLS models are examined in terms of R-squared, it is seen that the best OLS result is obtained with Multi-Linear Regression (0.946). Three-parameter OLS models result in terms of R-squared is given in **Table 2**.

The proximity between the predicted results of the model and the actual values measured with the Spirometer is shown in **Figure 7**. The results are quite close to each other. This figure shows the scattering of the predicted and actual values relative to each other. Accordingly, the blue dots on the figure show the data series linear regression situation.

The confusion matrix obtained from the results is given in **Table 3**. Overall accuracy was found at 93.3%. As a result, an efficient deep model is provided for estimating the VC parameter.

## 4. Discussion

The chapter aims to build an accurate and reliable deep neural network model to predict VC using weight, height, and age parameters (independent variables) as input

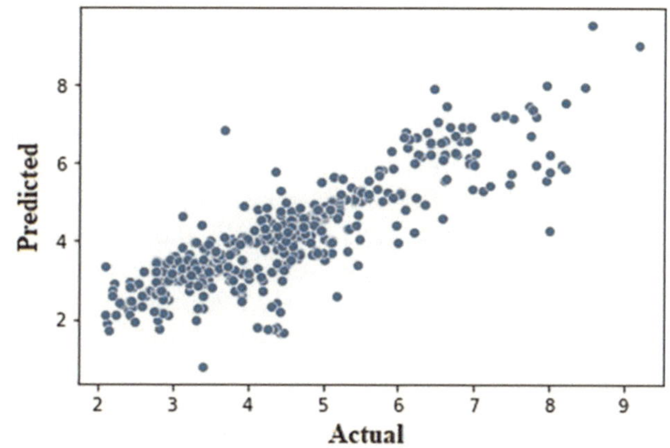


**Figure 7.**
*Evaluation of model performance.*

| A | P | |
|---|---|---|
| | **Predicted: Zero** | **Predicted: One** |
| **Actual: (Zero)** | 101 | 6 |
| **Actual: (One)** | 2 | 19 |

**Table 3.**
*The confusion matrix of the model.*

parameters to the model. The VC value (dependent variable) was taken as the output of the proposed deep neural network.

In this book chapter, a multiple-layer perceptron neural network (MLPFFNN) was selected as a preferred ANN algorithm. Three-parameter OLS models are examined in terms of R-squared, it is found that the best OLS result is obtained with Multi-Linear Regression (R-squared =0.948). The results showed that the height and age information has a significant effect on the VC compared to the weight information. These variables played a significant role in the prediction of VC. Although studies of estimating lung volume have been encountered in the literature search, a deep neural network model application that estimates the VC value using some specified independent parameters has not been found.

Therefore, it is believed that the results presented in this chapter will fill an important gap in the literature in light of both the database specificity and the presented ML-AI method.

## 5. Conclusions

COPD disease has become a challenging problem with the effect of COVID-19. The fact that the Respiratory Test Functions, which is the most effective method for diagnosing COPD, cannot be performed at home has forced researchers to find different, new, cheap, technological, and practical methods addressing this challenge.

In this book chapter, it is suggested that the deep neural network-based VC prediction algorithm can be used in clinical tests to reduce the workload of doctors and nurses. As shown in this chapter, a fast and reliable diagnostic tool using ML-AI algorithm was obtained. The proposed ML-AI model provided 93.3% accuracy. The simulation results showed that the VC parameter can be determined with a high success rate using the proposed deep learning model with real data. With the proposed model, the rate of misdiagnosis can be reduced and spirometric measurements can be made quickly without waiting for hours to have Pulmonary Function Test (PFT) performed in hospitals.

The simulation results indicate that a smart tool using ML-AI technology can be a reliable alternative to medical spirometers. Currently, the developed model is planned to be tested clinically and the results will be reported in future studies. The goal is to provide this smart tool to be used in hospitals after approval from field experts and governmental health agencies.

## Acknowledgements

This study is supported by the Coordinatorship of Ondokuz Mayıs University's Scientific Research Projects (Project Number: PYO.YMY.1901.20.001), Samsun,

Turkey. We would like to extend our heartfelt thanks to Dr. Kazım Sekeroğlu of Southeastern Louisiana University, Hammond, LA, USA.

## Conflict of interest

The authors declare no conflict of interest.

## Author details

Harun Sümbül
Yesilyurt D.C. Vocational School, Ondokuz Mayis University, Samsun, Turkey

*Address all correspondence to: harun.sumbul@omu.edu.tr

## References

[1] Fındık G, Aydoğdu K, Kaya S. Travma sonrası semptomatik hale gelen diyafram evantrasyonu. Turkish Journal of Thoracic and Cardiovascular Surgery. 2011;**19**(1):107-109

[2] Sümbül H, Yüzer AH. The measurement of COPD parameters (VC, RR, and FVC) by using Arduino embedded system. In: 1st International Mediterranean Science and Engineering Congress. Adana, Turkey: Çukurova University, Congress Center; 2016. pp. 201-207

[3] Sümbül H, Yüzer AH. Development of a diagnostic device for COPD: A MEMS based approach. International Journal of Computer Science and Network Security. 2017;**17**(7): 196-203

[4] Sümbül H, Yüzer AH. Measuring of diaphragm movements by using iMEMS acceleration sensor. In: International Conference on Electrical and Electronics Engineering. Bursa, Turkey: ELECO; 2015. pp. 166-170

[5] Irzaldy A, Wiyasihati SI, Purwanto B. Lung vital capacity of choir singers and nonsingers: A comparative study. Journal of Voice. 2016;**30**(6):717-720. DOI: 10.1016/j.jvoice.2015.08.008

[6] Tantucci C, Bottone D, Borghesi A, Guerini M, Quadri F, et al. Methods for measuring lung volumes: Is there a better one? Respiration. 2016;**91**(4):273-280. DOI: 10.1159/000444418

[7] Andrews JA, Meng L, Kulke SF, Rudnicki SA, Wolff AA, et al. Association between decline in slow vital capacity and respiratory insufficiency, use of assisted ventilation, tracheostomy, or death in patients with amyotrophic lateral sclerosis. JAMA Neurology. 2018; **75**(1):58-64. DOI: 10.1001/jamaneurol. 2017.3339

[8] Santos D B, Boré A, Castrillo LDA, Lacombe M, Falaize L, et al. Assisted vital capacity to assess recruitment level in neuromuscular diseases. Respiratory Physiology & Neurobiology 2017;**243**: 32-38. DOI: 10.1016/j.resp.2017.05.001

[9] Pellegrino GM, Papa GFS, Centanni S, Corbo M, Kvarnberg D, et al. Measuring vital capacity in amyotrophic lateral sclerosis: Effects of interfaces and reproducibility. Respiratory Medicine. 2021;**176**:106277. DOI: 10.1016/j.rmed. 2020.106277

[10] Brault M, Gabrysz-Forget F, Dubé BP. Predictive value of positional change in vital capacity to identify diaphragm dysfunction. Respiratory Physiology & Neurobiology. 2021;**289**: 103668. DOI: 10.1016/j.resp.2021.103668

[11] Calvo A, Vasta R, Moglia C, Matteoni E, Canosa A, et al. Prognostic role of slow vital capacity in amyotrophic lateral sclerosis. Journal of Neurology. 2020;**267**(6):1615-1621. DOI: 10.1007/s00415-020-09751-1

[12] "Vital Capacity". Family Practice Notebook. Retrieved February 19, 2015

[13] Bhatti U, Rani K, Memon MQ. Variation in lung volumes and capacities among young males in relation to height. Journal of Ayub Medical College, Abbottabad. 2014;**26**(2):200-202

[14] Sümbül H, Yüzer AH. Estimating the value of the volume from acceleration on the diaphragm movements during breathing. Journal of Engineering Science and Technology, School of Engineering, Taylor's University. 2018; **13**(5):1205-1221

[15] Pierce RJ, Brown DJ, Holmes M, Cumming G, Denison DM. Estimation of lung volumes from chest radiographs using shape information. Thorax. 1979;**34**(6):726-734. DOI: 10.1136/thx.34.6.726

[16] Lange B, Flynn S, Rizzo A, Bolas M, Silverman M, et al. Breath: A game to motivate the compliance of postoperative breathing exercises. In: Virtual Rehabilitation International Conference. Haifa, Israel: IEEE; 2009. pp. 94-97. DOI: 10.1109/ICVR.2009.5174212

[17] Yüzer AH, Sümbül H, Polat K. A novel wearable real-time sleep apnea detection system based on the acceleration sensor. IRBM. 2020;**41**(1): 39-47. DOI: 10.1016/j.irbm.2019.10.007

[18] Peters U, Kaminsky DA, Maksym GN. Chapter 2 - Standardized pulmonary function testing. In: Ionescu C, editor. Lung Function Testing in the 21st Century. London, UK: Academic Press; 2019. pp. 5-23. DOI: 10.1016/B978-0-12-814612-5.00002-6

[19] Sindi H, Nour M, Rawa M, Öztürk Ş, Polat K. An adaptive deep learning framework to classify unknown composite power quality event using known single power quality events. Expert Systems with Applications. 2021; **178**:115023. DOI: 10.1016/j.eswa.2021.115023

[20] LeCun Y, Bengio Y, Hinton G. Deep learning. Nature. 2015;**521**:436-444

[21] Yüzer AH, Sumbul H, Polat K, Nour M. A different sleep apnea classification system with neural network based on the acceleration signals. Applied Acoustics. 2020;**163**: 107225. DOI: 10.1016/j.apacoust.2020.107225

[22] Faust O, Hagiwara Y, Tan JH, Oh SL, Acharya UR. Deep learning for healthcare applications based on physiological signals: A review. Computer Methods and Programs in Biomedicine. 2018;**161**:1-13. DOI: 10.1016/j.cmpb.2018.04.005

[23] Uçar MK, Bozkurt MR, Bilgin C, et al. Automatic detection of respiratory arrests in OSA patients using PPG and machine learning techniques. Neural Computing and Applications. 2017;**28**:2931-2945. DOI: 10.1007/s00521-016-2617-9

[24] Uçar MK, Uçar Z, Uçar K, Akman M, Bozkurt MR. Determination of body fat percentage by electrocardiography signal with gender based artificial intelligence. Biomedical Signal Processing and Control. 2021;**68**: 102650. DOI: 10.1016/j.bspc.2021.102650

[25] Goodfellow I, Bengio Y, Courville A. Deep Learning. Cambridge, MA: The MIT Press; 2017

[26] Özkaya U, Seyfi L, Öztürk Ş. Dimension optimization of multi-band microstrip antennas using deep learning methods. Pamukkale University Journal of Engineering Sciences. 2021;**27**(2):229-233. DOI: 10.5505/pajes.2020.23471

[27] Ahmad I, Dar MA, Fenta A, Halefom A, Nega H, et al. Spatial configuration of groundwater potential zones using OLS regression method. Journal of African Earth Sciences. 2021; **177**:104147. DOI: 10.1016/j.jafrearsci.2021.104147

[28] Paletta A, Alimehmeti G, Mazzetti G, Guglielmi D. Educational leadership and innovative teaching practices: A polynomial regression and response surface analysis. International Journal of Educational Management. 2021. DOI: 10.1108/IJEM-01-2021-0019

[29] Chen D, Liu Y, Feng W, Wang Y,Hu Q, et al. In-situ prediction of α-phase volume fraction in titanium alloy using laser ultrasonic with support vector regression. Applied Acoustics. 2021;**177**: 107928. DOI:10.1016/j.apacoust. 2021.107928

[30] Liu Q, Wang F, Li J, Xiao W. A hybrid support vector regression with multi-domain features for low-velocity impact localization on composite plate structure. Mechanical Systems and Signal Processing. 2021;**154**:107547. DOI: 10.1016/j.ymssp.2020.107547

[31] Huo Y, Bouffard F, Joós G. Decision tree-based optimization for flexibility management for sustainable energy microgrids. Applied Energy. 2021;**290**: 116772. DOI: 10.1016/j.apenergy. 2021.116772

[32] Breiman L. Random forests. Machine Learning. 2001;**45**:5-32. DOI: 10.1023/A: 1010933404324

[33] Md Mujeeb S, Praveen Sam R, Madhavi K. Adaptive exponential Bat algorithm and deep learning for big data classification. Sådhanå. 2021;**46**:15. DOI: 10.1007/s12046-020-01521-z

Chapter 5

# Perspective Chapter: A Novel Method for Integrated Multicriteria Decision-Making with Uncertainty – A Case Study on Sustainable Agriculture in Colombia

*Marc Juanpera, Laia Ferrer-Martí, Marianna Garfí, Bruno Domenech and Rafael Pastor*

**Abstract**

Multicriteria decision-making usually requires a set of experts to evaluate the importance of selected criteria and the adequacy of feasible alternatives according to the criteria. Uncertainty can arise in these evaluations, since experts can be hesitant about their responses due to the difficulty of quantifying human language or lack of required knowledge. The Methodology for Integrated Multicriteria Decision-making with Uncertainty (MIMDU) tackles both factors of uncertainty by using non-predefined fuzzy numbers that are continuously adapted taking into account the level of confidence of the experts' opinions. The methodology also offers useful and complementary information to lead to a robust decision-making. This chapter proposes a novel methodology and provides a sample use case to demonstrate its capability to model uncertainty during decision-making process. In particular, a sensitivity analysis is included, which demonstrates (i) how uncertainty is incorporated into alternatives evaluation, and (ii) that the integrated multicriteria decision-making with uncertainty can be more reliable for decision-makers. The methodology is applied to the robust selection of the most sustainable technology to improve agriculture efficiency in rural areas by means of a case study of a low-cost biogas digester in a small-scale farm in Colombia.

**Keywords:** multicriteria decision-making, MIMDU methodology, confidence, rural areas development, sustainable agriculture

## 1. Introduction

Decision-making in industrial and service sectors usually requires selecting one of several feasible alternatives for a specific problem or situation. This selection is not an easy task, since different criteria (e.g., economic, technical, social, environmental, etc.) can be conflicting. Multicriteria decision-making is a suitable approach to handle such problems [1] and usually requires the participation of experts to weigh the criteria and to evaluate the feasible alternatives according to the selected criteria [2]. In particular, for decisions aiming at sustainable development, experts are required to take into account many conflicting criteria with very different nature. These criteria include but not limited to economic (e.g., implementation costs), technical (e.g., systems reliability, ease of maintenance), social (e.g., job creation, degree of acceptance over population), and environmental (e.g., particles emissions, waste generation). Thus, experts are required to evaluate alternatives across all the considered criteria requiring many different expertises. Uncertainties arise due to incomplete knowledge required from experts.

Indeed, experts' opinions are surrounded by two factors of uncertainty: (i) the potential lack of confidence when providing an answer [3], and (ii) the difficulty of quantifying the answer [4]. For example, one expert could hesitate on whether the importance of a criterion should be "high" or "low," and none of those answers has a clear and unequivocal quantification on a numeric scale. Literature has focused until now on the second factor, as proven by the wide use of Fuzzy Linguistic Scales (FLS) in many applications [5, 6]. With FLS, experts are required to choose from different terms (e.g., high or low importance of a criterion), which are quantified through fuzzy numbers (FN) equidistantly disposed along a numerical scale. As an example, **Figure 1** shows numerical scale from 0 to 5. Thus, the same fuzzy number is assigned to two experts considering the importance of a criterion should be, for example, "low," regardless of how confident they are with their answer (e.g., [8]). As it can be seen, such approach does not consider the potential lack of confidence of experts, who can be more informed about some criteria but less about others. Thus, the developed MIMDU presented in this chapter addresses a research gap by considering the lack of confidence in human opinions.

The proposed MIMDU methodology can be used to enhance the efficiency of rural agriculture. As an example, the technique is used to increase the quality of a biofertilizer in developing farm areas with biogas digesters. Such biogas digesters

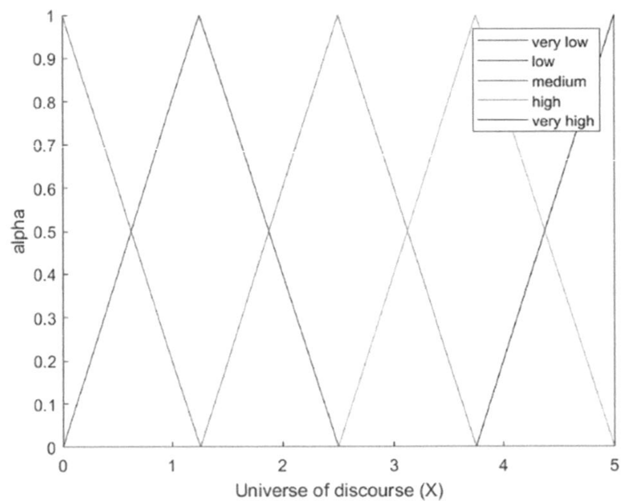


**Figure 1.**
*Usual modeling of FN in literature [7].*

degrade cattle manure in anaerobic conditions to produce biogas for cooking or heating and a liquid effluent called digestate [9]. Digestate can be used as a biofertilizer, but it needs to be posttreated for its safe and efficient application to agricultural soil [10].

Different low-tech and low-cost alternatives, coupled with the digesters, can be implemented to posttreat the digestate. In this chapter, the following common posttreatment alternatives are considered to be feasible in a rural context and to allow the stabilization of the organic matter and the reduction of pathogens concentration: (i) a degassing tank, (ii) a sand filter, (iii) a vermifilter, (iv) digestate recirculation in the digester, and (v) a facultative pond. Most of these posttreatment technologies have been studied mainly for the treatment of urban wastewater [11, 12], and only a few studies were carried out with digestates. In this case, a comparative study of alternatives for the posttreatment of digestate from low-tech digesters is missing.

In this context, the aim of this chapter is twofold. First, to demonstrate the novelty of MIMDU to robustly assist multicriteria decision-making considering hesitance in human responses. Second, to apply MIMDU to select the best alternative for digestate posttreatment before its sustainable use in agriculture to enhance crop production. Sesction 2 details the phases of MIMDU, Section 3 provides an example case for illustrative purposes, displays the results of the case study in Colombia, and Section 3 concludes the MIMDU work presented in this chapter.

## 2. Methodology for integrated multicriteria decision-making with uncertainty (MIMDU)

This section aims to present the process defined by MIMDU, detailing its three phases along with an example case to ease understanding. The three phases include modeling opinions, alternatives ranking, and results interpretation. For comprehension purpose, the example considers a small number of alternatives (e.g., 3) and criteria (e.g., 3), although real case studies can take into account larger numbers of alternatives and criteria, as seen in Section 3. The application of the third phase in the example case is complemented with a sensitivity analysis that aims to show the potential of MIMDU to assist decision-making. Next, the three phases are discussed as follows:

**P1. Modeling Opinions**: Triangular fuzzy numbers (TFNs) are used in the form of fuzzy rating scales to continuously define the shape of the TFN through intuitive questions gathering the experts' hesitance [13]. Two steps are defined in this phase:

Step 1: The expert must choose a value on a 0–5 scale to rate the importance of a criterion (high value means high importance of the criterion) and to evaluate an alternative according to a criterion (high value means high adequacy of the alternative to the criterion).

Step 2: The expert must express his/her confidence with the reference value expressed in Step 1, from five options presented in **Table 1**. The more confident the expert is, the lower "*support*" (base of the TFN) will have in the answer quantification, and the less vague the quantification will be.

Example case:

This example considers three experts assessing the importance of the three criteria shown in **Table 2**. The adequacy of each alternative according to each criterion is

| Confidence in the response | Relative support |
|---|---|
| Completely sure (CS) | 0% |
| Sure (S) | 15% |
| Indecisive (I) | 30% |
| Unsure (U) | 45% |
| Very unsure (VU) | 60% |

**Table 1.**
*Options to express the level of confidence and quantify the support of the TFN [7].*

| Criteria | Expert | Importance | Confidence |
|---|---|---|---|
| C1 | E1 | 3 | S |
| | E2 | 4 | I |
| | E3 | 1 | VU |
| C2 | E1 | 2 | U |
| | E2 | 4 | S |
| | E3 | 4 | I |
| C3 | E1 | 3 | S |
| | E2 | 3 | VU |
| | E3 | 5 | U |

**Table 2.**
*Experts' evaluations of the importance of the criteria [7].*

presented in **Table 3**. In both processes, namely rating the importance of the criteria and evaluating the alternatives according to the criteria, each expert first provides a reference value on a 0–5 scale and the associated confidence level, from the options in **Table 1**.

For instance, **Figure 2** illustrates the importance given by the three experts (E1, E2, E3) to C1: E1 is sure on the importance with a score 3 out of 5, E2 is indecisive about it with a score of 4, and E3 rates with a 1 but is very unsure.

This approach establishes a more precise modeling of opinions compared with literature, since TFNs are not defined beforehand. Such flexibility allows to quantify the experts' level of confidence (Step 2) and defines several confidence levels associated with the answers from experts, i.e., concrete or vague answers. The confidence levels have a decisive influence on the ranking of the final alternatives, as shown in Phase 3 (P3) below. Different confidence levels allow the experts to express their potential lack of confidence, which may also reduce the pressure felt by experts when answering, especially in scenarios of limited knowledge or high uncertainty.

**P2. Alternatives Ranking**: The Compromise Ranking Method (CRM) is used to calculate a final FN for each alternative as an indicator of how good the alternative is compared with the others. For the CRM, this indicator is the distance of each alternative to an ideal solution, which determines the best of all the alternatives across selected criteria [14]. The best alternative will be the one with the lower distance to the ideal solution, which is an utopian solution that performs optimally (achieving the best evaluations) for all the criteria considered [7]. In particular, MIMDU includes a

| Criteria | Expert | A1 | | A2 | | A3 | |
|---|---|---|---|---|---|---|---|
| | | Evaluation (Eval.) | Confidence (Conf.) | Eval. | Conf. | Eval. | Conf. |
| C1 | E1 | 3 | S | 2 | U | 1 | U |
| | E2 | 3 | U | 2 | VU | 3 | VU |
| | E3 | 4 | U | 4 | CS | 5 | S |
| C2 | E1 | 1 | VU | 1 | S | 5 | U |
| | E2 | 2 | CS | 2 | I | 4 | S |
| | E3 | 4 | S | 2 | S | 3 | S |
| C3 | E1 | 2 | I | 1 | I | 3 | CS |
| | E2 | 3 | VU | 2 | U | 3 | S |
| | E3 | 5 | U | 3 | S | 2 | I |

**Table 3.**
*Experts' evaluations of the adequacy of alternatives according to criteria [7].*

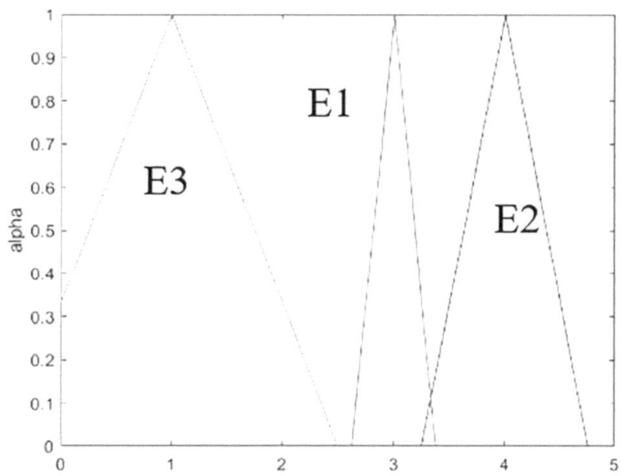


**Figure 2.**
*Modeling of the importance given by the three experts to C1.*

fuzzy version of the CRM (F-CRM), represented in Eqs. (1) and (2), using α-cut intervals. Thus, each FN is represented as a sequence of a discrete number of intervals for different cuts (from the bottom $\alpha$ =0, to the top $\alpha$ =1) according to different values of $\alpha$. The reader is referred to [7] for an exhaustive explanation of the α-cut arithmetic.

$$^{\alpha}L_{i,p} = \left[\sum_{j=1}^{n}\left({}^{\alpha}W_j\right)^p \cdot \left(\frac{{}^{\alpha}F_j^* - {}^{\alpha}f_{ij}}{{}^{\alpha}F_j^* - {}^{\alpha}f_j^*}\right)^p\right]^{1/p} \tag{1}$$

$$^{\alpha}L_i = 0.5 \cdot {}^{\alpha}L_{i,1} + 0.5 \cdot {}^{\alpha}L_{i,\infty} \tag{2}$$

Where ${}^{\alpha}L_{i,p}$ is defined as the standardized distance of each alternative $i$ to the ideal solution for a given metric $p$, and ${}^{\alpha}L_i$ is the final distance to the ideal solution and constitutes the final score of the alternative $i$ and allows it to be ranked. In particular, for each value of $\alpha$, ${}^{\alpha}W_j$ is the weight of criterion $j$ (an average of opinions on the importance of criterion $j$ by all experts consulted); ${}^{\alpha}f_{ij}$ is the evaluation of alternative $i$ according to criterion $j$ (also an average of all experts consulted); ${}^{\alpha}F_j^*$ and ${}^{\alpha}f_j^*$ are the best and the worst values obtained, respectively, for any alternative on criterion $j$, and $p$ is a metric used to calculate different distances to the ideal solution (as mentioned above, the one that ideally achieves the best values for all the criteria). An average (${}^{\alpha}L_i$) is calculated from the two usual and extreme metrics, $p$ =1, for maximum global utility (${}^{\alpha}L_{i,1}$) and $p$ =∞, for the minimum individual regret (${}^{\alpha}L_{i,\infty}$) [15].

Example case:

Applying Eqs. (1) and (2) for 11 values of α (from 0 to 1 with a step size of 0.1), the results of the distance to the ideal solution for each alternative (${}^{\alpha}L_i$) are shown in **Figure 3**. As it can be seen, all alternatives have distances to the ideal solution above 0. Intuitively, it seems that A1 and A3 achieve lower distances than A2, so the latter could be discarded. However, the "Results Interpretation" phase is useful to discuss which one is the best (minor distance), since fuzzy numbers are clearly overlap in this example.

**P3. Results Interpretation**: As mentioned in P2, ranking alternatives from their fuzzy values might be misleading (e.g., in the above example, it is not clear if A1 or A3 achieve a lower fuzzy distance to the ideal solution). Thus, a comparison of a crisp ranking and a fuzzy-based ranking is proposed:

Crisp ranking: it is determined by the results of ${}^{1}L_i$, which does not consider the experts' level of confidence, but only the numerical values responded by the experts in Step 1. This deterministic ranking is intrinsically significant and meant the only decision-aid source in relevant studies of the literature [2, 16].

Fuzzy-based: The Middle Point of the Mean Interval (MPMI) described in Eq. (3) is used to calculate the best non-fuzzy performance value of each final FN (${}^{\alpha}L_i$) [17].

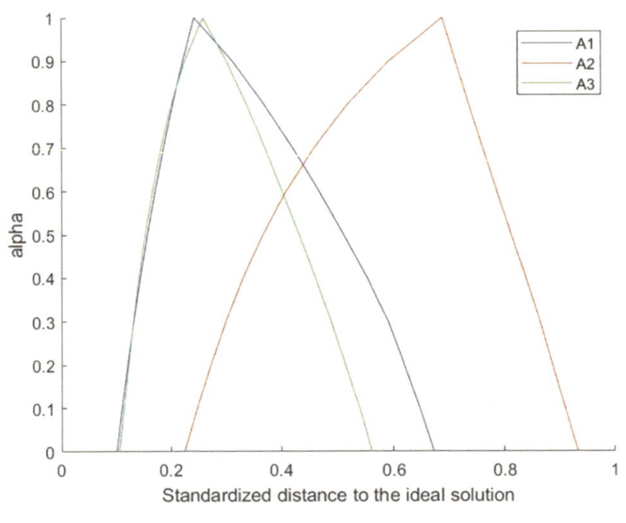


**Figure 3.**
*FN for the distance of A1–A3 to the ideal solution [7].*

This method integrates, for each alternative, the average of the lowest and highest value for each $\alpha$-cut interval of the distance of the alternative to the ideal solution:

$$\mathrm{MPMI_i} = \int_0^1 \frac{\min\ {}^{\alpha}\mathrm{L_i} + \max\ {}^{\alpha}\mathrm{L_i}}{2} d\alpha \tag{3}$$

Example case:

**Table 4** shows both the crisp ranking and the fuzzy-based values that can be used to rank the alternatives. As shown in **Table 4**, the two rankings diverge. According to the crisp ranking, the best alternative would be A1 (lower distance to the ideal solution), followed by A3 and A2, i.e., A1-A3-A2. These results can be observed at the top of **Figure 3** (only values for $\alpha$ =1). However, for the fuzzy-based ranking, which considers the level of confidence of the experts, the ranking of the alternatives would be A3-A1-A2. The difference occurs because A1 has been better evaluated than A3 by the experts when expressing numerical values for their adequacy to each criterion (Step 1), but at the same time, they expressed a lower level of confidence (Step 2). Oppositely, A3 has been evaluated slightly worse, but more confidently, which eventually can make A3 a more reliable choice when assessing the whole experts' opinions.

In line with this discussion, and in order to fully show the potential of MIMDU to assist decision-making, a sensitivity analysis was carried out by modifying the evaluations of A3 according to C3 performed by expert E3. In particular, it is considered that this expert evaluates A3 according to C3 with the same reference value of 2 as shown in the last row of **Table 3**. But for this case, it evaluates A3 with the five options of confidence levels: CS, S, I, U, VU (i.e., five scenarios), instead of only the original I. **Table 5** shows the non-fussy performance value of the distance of alternative A3 to the ideal solution ($MPMI_{A3}$) for all confidence scenarios. It can be seen that the lowest distance, and thus the best ranking-value of alternative A3, is obtained when E3 is completely sure (CS) of their evaluation of A3. Meanwhile, the worst ranking-value of A3 is achieved when he/she is very unsure (VU) of the evaluation. This result is consistent with the process detailed and is understandable, since more confidently evaluated alternatives are achieving better ranking results.

Those two extreme values ($MPMI_{A3}$ when the expert is CS and when he/she is VU) can be compared with $MPMI_{A1}$, which remains unchanged, i.e., when $MPMI_{A3}$ in the VU confidence case is 9.42% lower than the one for A1 (0.298 against 0.329; **Tables 4** and 5, respectively); it increases up to 11.85% lower for the CS case (0.290 against 0.329; **Tables 4** and 5, respectively). This means there is a difference of

| | A1 | A2 | A3 |
|---|---|---|---|
| Crisp: ${}^{1}L_i$ | **0.243** | 0.689 | 0.259 |
| Fuzzy-based: $MPMI_i$ | 0.329 | 0.603 | **0.294** |

**Table 4.**
*Crisp and fuzzy rankings of the alternatives in the example case [7].*

| E3 | CS | S | I (original) | U | VU |
|---|---|---|---|---|---|
| $MPMI_{A3}$ | 0.290 | 0.292 | 0.294 | 0.296 | 0.298 |

**Table 5.**
*Sensitivity analysis on the hesitance on the evaluation of A3 for E3.*

25.80% (11.85 vs. 9.42%) between the distances of A1 and A3 with only one expert changing the level of confidence of the evaluation. It seems then that the level of confidence plays an important role in the final ranking of the alternatives, in which alternatives evaluated more confidently, such as A3 stands out.

## 3. Application: selection of the best alternative for digestate posttreatment for low-cost digesters in small-scale farms

This section describes the application of MIMDU to select the best alternative to posttreat the digestate before its sustainable use as a biofertilizer in agriculture.

### 3.1 Alternatives presentation and criteria definition

Five low-tech alternatives are considered to treat the digestate obtained in a low-cost biogas digester implemented in a small farm in Colombia. As shown in **Figure 4**, all alternatives are implemented just after the biogas digester to posttreat the digestate. The five alternatives are given below:

- A1. Degassing tank alternative: It allows the recovery of the remaining diluted methane and stabilizes the organic matter producing more biogas.

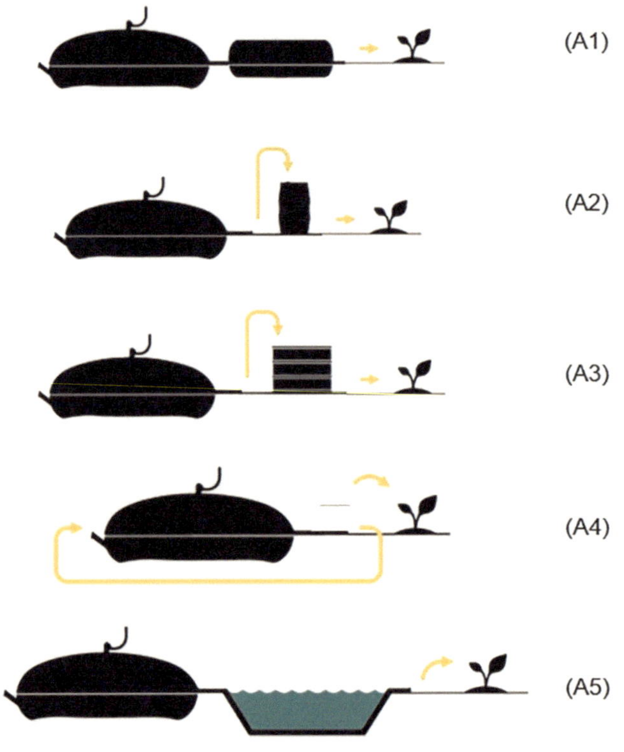


**Figure 4.**
*Five alternatives for digestate posttreatment, Adapted from [18].*

- A2. Sand filter alternative: It employs both physical and biological processes, without energy outputs, to reduce the digestate turbidity and remove suspended solids and pathogens.

- A3. Vermifilter alternative: It consists of a biofilter with earthworms that helps to accelerate the decomposition of organic matter. The earthworms' activity increases the porosity of the fertilizer obtained from the organic matter, called vermicompost, creating aerobic conditions that avoid the emission of unpleasant odors.

- A4. Digestate alternative: Recirculation into the digester. This is a simple solution that allows recovering the diluted methane and stabilizes the organic matter while saving water.

- A5. Facultative pond alternative: It can be a shallow basin that aims to remove pathogens and ammonia nitrogen, as well as treating the effluent. Facultative ponds benefit from high solar radiation, which enhances bacterial activity.

Also, combining alternatives in series (e.g., A1 + A2, A1 + A3, and A1 + A5) has been also considered for their complementary nature. Other combinations were not realistic in practice for small farms in rural areas.

These five alternatives are evaluated according to 10 criteria and 22 (sub)criteria (**Table 6**), selected after discussion with experts in the field and divided into three categories, namely technical, environmental, and socioeconomic [19]. The categories are defined as follows:

- Technical criteria (T) aim to assess the suitability of the posttreated digestate for agriculture, which demands a reduced amount of heavy metals and pathogens and a high content of dry matter, organic matter, and nutrients. They also take into account the adaptability of the alternative to the context of small-scale farms in countries with low income, stating how easy to manage they are, the area they require, and their expected lifetime.

- Environmental (E) criteria focus on evaluating the impact of the alternatives for digestate posttreatment. The criteria include air pollution (emission of particles, greenhouse gases, and odors) and the resources they consume (whether they use sustainable and local materials, and the amount of water and energy demanded).

- Socioeconomic (S) criteria study the possible harmful and benefitting consequences of the alternatives in the everyday life of the population. It considers aspects such as the cost of implementation and maintenance, the potential income generation and savings it can provide for the families (for example, due to improved agriculture production), and the social acceptance of the population, which can be based on positive or negative past experiences.

### 3.2 Modeling uncertainty

A total of 16 experts from the network for Biodigesters in Latin America and the Caribbean (RedBioLAC, 2020 edition) participated in a survey to define the importance of each criterion using the MIMDU procedure. As an example, the assessments

| Aspects | Criteria | | Sub-criteria | | E1 | | E2 | | ... | E16 | |
|---|---|---|---|---|---|---|---|---|---|---|---|
| | | | | | Eval. | Conf. | Eval. | Conf. | | Eval. | Conf. |
| **Technical** | T1 | Digestate characteristics | T1.1 | Heavy metals content | 3 | U | 2 | I | ... | 5 | U |
| | | | T1.2 | Pathogens content | 3 | I | 3 | I | | 5 | U |
| | | | T1.3 | Dry matter content | 2 | I | 3 | VU | | 2 | I |
| | | | T1.4 | Organic matter content | 2 | I | 3 | VU | | 2 | I |
| | | | T1.5 | Nutrients content | 4 | S | 4 | I | | 4 | I |
| | | | T1.6 | Diluted biomethane | 4 | VS | 4 | VS | | 4 | I |
| | T2 | Management | T2.1 | Skilled labor | 4 | S | 5 | VS | | 3 | S |
| | | | T2.2 | Ease of construction and maintenance | 3 | S | 3 | S | | 5 | I |
| | | | T2.3 | Ease of maintenance | 4 | S | 3 | VS | | 5 | I |
| | T3 | Surface area requirement | — | Surface area requirement | 3 | S | 2 | U | | 5 | U |
| | T4 | Lifespan | — | Lifespan | 4 | S | 4 | VU | | 5 | U |
| **Environmental** | E1 | Air pollution | E1.1 | Emission of particulate matter, greenhouse gases and sulfur oxides | 3 | I | 4 | VS | | 4 | I |
| | | | E1.2 | Emission of odors | 3 | I | 5 | VS | | 4 | S |
| | E2 | Resources consumption | E2.1 | Sustainability of materials | 4 | S | 3 | U | | 5 | S |
| | | | E2.2 | Water consumption | 4 | S | 3 | I | | 5 | S |
| | | | E2.3 | Energy consumption | 4 | S | 2 | VU | | 3 | I |
| **Socio-economic** | S1 | Costs | S1.1 | Initial investment | 4 | S | 5 | S | | 5 | VS |
| | | | S1.2 | Maintenance costs | 4 | S | 3 | VS | | 5 | S |
| | S2 | Benefits | S2.1 | Income generation | 4 | S | 2 | I | | 5 | S |
| | | | S2.2 | Savings | 3 | I | 1 | VU | | 5 | VS |
| | S3 | Standard of living | S3 | Equity and standard of living | 4 | I | 3 | VU | | 5 | VS |
| | S4 | Social acceptance | S4 | Social acceptance | 4 | S | 5 | VS | | 5 | VS |

**Table 6.**
*Criteria and subcriteria defined and evaluation of their importance.*

of three experts are shown in **Table 6**, reflecting their differences according to the technical or academic background of each expert (E1 and E2 have industry technical background and E16 has academic training). When looking at the socioeconomic criteria, it is observed that experts E1 and E2 evaluated their importance with less confidence level than E16, who is either sure or very sure (S and VS) of their high importance. Oppositely, E16 has different opinions on the importance of the technical criteria (for example, he/she assigns a 5 to the digestate content of heavy metals and pathogens, and a 2 to the dry, organic matter and nutrients contents), but is in all cases indecisive (I) and unsure (U) about the evaluations. Hence, the use of MIMDU allows to capture that uncertainty and modeling the responses consequently.

Regarding the evaluations of the alternatives, the uncertainty modeling is tackled differently according to the quantitative and qualitative nature of each (sub)criterion, and they are given below.

Quantitative (sub)criteria are T1, T3, T4, E2.2, E2.3, and S1. For these (sub) criteria, a reference value of the evaluations is obtained with real data collected in situ. Such real data embraced parameters of the construction and operation of the full-scale digesters in Colombia (e.g., biogas production and quality characteristics of the digestate, including heavy metals, pathogens, organic matter, nutrients, etc.). On the other hand, the impact of the alternatives on those digestate parameters, such as reduction rates for the metal or pathogens content, and increase rates for the dry, organic matter and nutrients, are taken from the literature [11, 20, 21]. The alternatives are also sized (determining the surface and volume required to process the digestate coming from the biogas digester, and the materials needed) to obtain an initially estimated of the initial investment and maintenance cost from the amount of materials needed in each alternative. Finally, to define a TFN, a 10% deviation from the reference value is considered to account for uncertainty on the inherent data obtained. This 10% was agreed among the experts involved in the decision-making as an appropriate estimation of the deviation of measures of biogas digester's and digestate's parameters. The specific detail of the evaluation of the alternatives according to the quantitative (sub)criteria for the specific case study can be found in [19].

Qualitative (sub)criteria are T2, E1, E2.1, S2, S3, and S4. For these (sub)criteria, a similar procedure explained in Section 2 is used to evaluate the alternatives. An assessment of 0–5 is assigned to each pair alternative-criterion according to how much the alternative fulfills the criterion, and a $\pm 1$ deviation is considered to account for the potential uncertainty in the human judgment due to hesitance. Similarly, specific details of the evaluation of the alternatives according to the qualitative (sub)criteria can be found in [19].

### 3.3 Alternatives ranking and discussion

From the experts' opinions on the criteria weights and the evaluations of the alternatives, the F-CRM is applied using Eqs. (1) and (2), and the corresponding MPMI is calculated for each alternative. **Table 7** shows the results of the crisp and the fuzzy-based ranking of all the alternatives considered for digestate post-treatment in small-scale farms located in rural. The vermifilter (A3) appears to be the best posttreatment alternative for both rankings, followed by recirculation (A4) and sand filtration (A2) alternatives. The similarity between the crisp and fuzzy rankings confirms the robustness of the results, since it means that the uncertainty included in both weights and evaluations does not modify the result achieved due to the crisp opinions

| | A1 | A2 | A3 | A4 | A5 | A1 + A2 | A1 + A3 | A1 + A5 |
|---|---|---|---|---|---|---|---|---|
| ${}^{1}L_i$ | 0.348 | 0.309 | **0.186** | 0.272 | 0.406 | 0.414 | 0.331 | 0.486 |
| Crisp ranking | 5 | 3 | **1** | 2 | 6 | 7 | 4 | 8 |
| $MPMI_i$ | 0.358 | 0.293 | **0.213** | 0.288 | 0.394 | 0.391 | 0.329 | 0.450 |
| Fuzzy-based ranking | 5 | 3 | **1** | 2 | 7 | 6 | 4 | 8 |

**Table 7.**
*Crisp and fuzzy rankings of the alternatives for digestate post-treatment [19].*

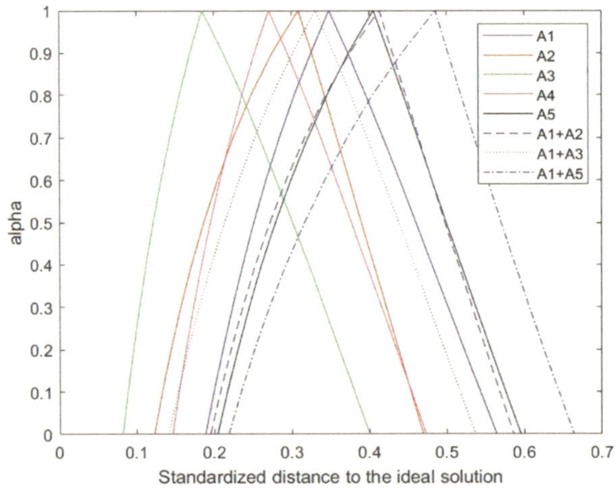


**Figure 5.**
*FN for the distance of A1 – A1 + A5 to the ideal solution [19].*

of experts. **Figure 5** offers a representation of the FN and is in accordance with the conclusions provided. The results show that the distance of A3 to the ideal solution is clearly lower than the others alternatives, i.e., the corresponding FN is placed more to the left. These results should ease and increase the confidence of decision-makers.

The overall predominance of the vermifilter alternative (A3) relies on its capacity of generating a final product (vermicompost), which is easier to implement, manage, and transport, and at the same time, it is a high-quality biofertilizer that can increase the agriculture production and has itself market potential for being sold [22]. In consequence, it accounts for the best evaluation in some of the environmental and socioeconomic criteria, such as the sustainability of materials needed for its implementation (basically wood, E2.1) and its capacity of generating income for the beneficiary population (S2.1). Alternatively, coupling a degassing tank and a vermifilter in series (i.e., combined A1 and A3, a.k.a. A1 + A3) enhances even more the quality of the digestate, since diluted methane is highly recovered (T1.6), but represents significantly greater economic investments for implementation and day-to-day operation.

Other well-ranked alternatives are recirculating the digestate alternative (A4) and implementing a sand filter alternative (A2). A4 is very easy to implement, does not require skilled labor (T2.1, T2.2) nor surface area (T3), and reduces the amount of water that feeds the digester (E2.2). Meanwhile, A2 drastically reduces the heavy metals content (T1.1) and has a long life span (T4).

## 4. Conclusions

MIMDU is a novel Methodology for Integrated Multicriteria Decision-Making with Uncertainty that focuses on integrating the experts' level of confidence into their responses. The method is divided into three phases, namely modeling opinions (P1), ranking alternatives (P2), and interpreting the results (P3). Compared with other multicriteria methods available in the literature (such as VIKOR and TOPSIS [1]), MIMDU offers two key features, including (1) generate better estimation of the opinions collected from experts incorporating their various levels of confidence through predefined TFN, and (2) provide complimentary information for a robust decision-making, including a crisp ranking without uncertainty consideration and a fuzzy-based ranking incorporated uncertainty considerations. These MIMDU's features enable a robust decision-making process.

To ease comprehension, MIMDU was demonstrated for a generic example case with reduced size. An example using three criteria and three alternatives was provided. Results obtained from this example showed that the proposed MIMDU procedure helps decision-makers to choose the most reliable alternative, as significant differences in the ranking "without" and "with uncertainty" can be quantified and compared. Specifically, for the example use case, the crisp ranking showed that alternative A1 is 6.58% better than alternative A3; but when the level of confidence is considered, A3 turns out to be 10.64% better; and hence A3 is selected as the best alternative as compared with A1 and A2. Also, the effect of lower or higher confidence in the response is tackled within a sensitivity analysis. Results show that increasing the confidence when evaluating an alternative can significantly improve its performance in the final ranking.

Finally, the proposed MIMDU was demonstrated for digestate posttreatment in small-scale farms with low-cost biodigesters. Both the crisp and fuzzy-based ranking results pointed out that the vermifilter alternative is the best option, followed by recirculating the digestate and the sand filter alternatives. In particular, the vermifilter is confirmed as an environmental-friendly technology that is allowed to create a high-quality product (vermicompost) to increase agricultural productivity and also generate incomes to the families due to sales. The consideration of uncertainty in both the experts' opinions and the alternatives evaluation demonstrated that MIMDU is a robust decision-making method for agriculture applications. The proposed MIMDU procedure described in this chapter can be extended to other applications.

## Acknowledgements

This research was possible thanks to the grant FPU18/05389 and the research project RTI2018-097962-B-I00, funded by the Spanish Ministry of Science, Innovation and Universities MCIN/AEI/10.13039/501100011033 and FEDER. The research was cofunded by the UPC Centre for Development Cooperation (CCD2021-G006).

## Conflict of interest

The authors declare no conflict of interest.

## Author details

Marc Juanpera[1]*, Laia Ferrer-Martí[2], Marianna Garfí[3], Bruno Domenech[1] and Rafael Pastor[1]

1 Department of Management, Universitat Politècnica de Catalunya—BarcelonaTECH, Spain

2 Department of Mechanical Engineering, Universitat Politècnica de Catalunya—BarcelonaTECH, Spain

3 Department of Civil and Environmental Engineering, Universitat Politècnica de Catalunya—BarcelonaTECH, Spain

*Address all correspondence to: marc.juanpera@upc.edu

## References

[1] Opricovic S, Tzeng G. Compromise solution by MCDM methods: A comparative analysis of VIKOR and TOPSIS. European Journal of Operational Research. 2004;**156**:445-455. DOI: 10.1016/S0377-2217(03)00020-1

[2] Domenech B, Ferrer-Martí L, Pastor R. Hierarchical Methodology to Optimize the Design of Stand-Alone Electrification Systems for Rural Communities considering Technical and Social Criteria. Renewable and Sustainable Energy Reviews. 2015;**51**: 182-196. DOI: 10.1016/j.rser.2015.06.017

[3] Chen S-M, Hong J-A. Multicriteria linguistic decision making based on hesitant fuzzy linguistic term sets and the aggregation of fuzzy sets. Information Sciences. 2014;**286**:63-74. DOI: 10.1016/j.ins.2014.06.020

[4] Zadeh LA. The concept of a linguistic variable and its application to approximate reasoning - I. Information Sciences. 1975;**8**:199-249. DOI: 10.1016/ 0020-0255(75)90036-5

[5] Abdel-Baset M, Chang V, Gamal A, Smarandache F. An Integrated Neutrosophic ANP and VIKOR Method for Achieving Sustainable Supplier Selection: A Case Study in importing Field. Computers in Industry. 2019;**106**: 94-11. DOI: 10.1016/j.compind.2018. 12.017

[6] Rostamzadeh R, Govindan K, Esmaeili A, Sabaghi M. Application of fuzzy VIKOR for evaluation of green supply chain management practices. Renewable and Sustainable Energy Reviews. 2015;**51**:182-196. DOI: 10.1016/ j.ecolind.2014.09.045

[7] Juanpera M, Domenech B, Ferrer-Martí L, García-Villoria A, Pastor R. Methodology for Integrated Multicriteria Decision-Making with Uncertainty: Extending the Compromise Ranking Method for Uncertain Evaluation of Alternatives. Fuzzy Sets and Systems. 2022;**2022**(434):135-158. DOI: 10.1016/ j.fss.2021.08.008

[8] Shojaie AA, Babaie S, Sayah E, Mohammaditabar D. Analysis and Prioritization of Green Health Suppliers Using Fuzzy ELECTRE Method with a Case Study. Global Journal of Flexible Systems Management. 2018;**19**:39-52. DOI: 10.1007/s40171-017-0168-2

[9] Ferrer I, Garfí M, Uggetti E, Ferrer L, Calderon A, Velo E. Biogas production in low-cost household digesters at the Peruvian Andes. Biomass and Bioenergy. 2011;**35**(5):1668-1674. DOI: 10.1016/ j.biombioe.2010.12.036

[10] Garfi M, Martí-Herrero J, Garwood A, Ferrer I. Household anaerobic digesters for biogas production in Latin America: A review. Renewable and Sustainable Energy Reviews. 2016;**60**:599-614. DOI: 10.1016/j.rser.2016.01.071

[11] Patil PM, Husain M. Enhancing Efficiency of Anaerobic Digestion by Sand Filtration of Effluent. American Journal of Environmental Engineering. 2019;**9**(1):12-15. DOI: 0.5923/j.ajee.2019 0901.03

[12] Krishnasamy K, Nair J, Hughes RJ. Vermifiltration systems for liquid waste management: A review. International Journal of Environment and Waste Management. 2013;**12**:4. DOI: 10.1504/ ijewm.2013.056908

[13] Lubiano MA, Rosa de Sáa S, Montenegro M, Sinova B, Gil MA.

Descriptive Analysis of Responses to Items in Questionnaires. Why not Using a Fuzzy Rating Scale? Information Sciences. 2016;**360**:131-148. DOI: 10.1016/j.ins.2016.04.029

[14] Zeleny M. Compromise programming. Multiple criteria decision making. Columbia: University of South Carolina Press; 1973. pp. 263-301

[15] Yücenur GN, Demirel NÇ. Group decision making process for insurance company selection problem with extended VIKOR method under fuzzy environment. Expert Systems with Applications. 2012;**39**:3702-3707. DOI: 10.1016/j.eswa.2011.09.065

[16] Ferrer-Martí L, Ferrer I, Sánchez E, Garfí M. A multi-criteria decision support tool for the assessment of household biogas digester programmes in rural areas. A case study in Peru. Renewable and Sustainable Energy Reviews. 2018;**95**:74-83. DOI: 10.1016/j.rser.2018.06.064

[17] Dubois D. Possibility Theory and Statistical Reasoning. Computational Statistics and Data Analysis. 2006;**51**:47-69. DOI: 10.1016/j.csda.2006.04.015

[18] Monteagudo S. Desarrollo de un análisis multicriterio para la selección de alternativas sostenibles para el postratamiento del efluente de biodigestores de bajo coste [thesis]. Barcelona, Spain: Universitat Politècnica de Catalunya; 2020

[19] Juanpera M, Ferrer-Martí L, Diez-Montero R, Ferrer I, Castro L, Escalante H, et al. A robust multicriteria analysis for the post-treatment of digestate from low-tech digesters. Boosting the circular bioeconomy of small-scale farms in Colombia. Renewable and Sustainable Energy Reviews. 2022;**166**:112638

[20] Mara D. Domestic Wasterwater Treatment in Developing Countries. Earthscan; 2003. p. 311. ISBN: 1-84407-019-0. Available at: https://www.pseau.org/outils/ouvrages/earthscan_ltd_domestic_wastewater_treatment_in_developing_countries_2003.pdf

[21] Garg P, Gupta A, Satya S. Vermicomposting of different types of waste using Eisenia foetida: A comparative study. Bioresource Technology. 2006;**97**:391-395. DOI: 10.1016/j.biortech.2005.03.009

[22] Kannadasan N, Balasubramanian B, Palanisamy T, Shanmugam S, Pushparaj K, Al-Dhabi NA, et al. Sustainable biotreatment of textile dye effluent water by using earthworms through vermifiltration. Journal of King Saud University – Science. 2021;**33**:101615. DOI: 10.1016/j.jksus.2021.101615

Section 3

# Optimization Modeling in Decision Science

Chapter 6

# Satisficing Decision-Making

*Andrzej Łodziński*


## Abstract

The chapter presents a decision support system. The decision-making process is modeled by a multi-criteria optimization problem. The decision support method is an interactive decision-making process. The choice is made by solving the problem depending on the control parameters that define the aspirations of the decision makers for each criteria function, then it evaluates the obtained solution by accepting or rejecting it. In another case, the decision maker selects a new value and the problem is solved again for the new parameter. In this chapter, an example of a decision support system is presented.


**Keywords:** multi-criteria optimization, efficient decision, scalarizing function, method of decision selection, decision support system

## 1. Introduction

Decision support systems are a very broad field, including theoretical approaches and methods of their application [1–14]. Decision support involves the automation of certain steps in the decision-making process. The extent of such automation is an important issue. Methods that provide a high degree of automation of the decision-making process are optimization methods of decision support based on value and utility theory that use analytical forms of decision situation models and expert systems in decision support, related to artificial intelligence and knowledge engineering and using logical forms of models. The practice and psychology of decision support prefer a different approach based on emphasizing the sovereign role of the decision maker, assuming that he can be assisted by automation of some stages of the decision-making process but should sovereignly and fully consciously make the final choice of decision.

A decision is usually called a choice between multiple possibilities. The person making the decision is usually referred to as the decision maker. The issue of preparing and making a decision is usually much more complex than, as the above definition of the term decision would suggest, the mere problem of choosing between some options. Initially, we usually do not know the decision options, thus, we have to prepare or generate them on our own; the very issue of preparing decision options is often complex and usually more time-consuming than the issue of choice. However, before we start preparing options, we often do not even know our exact point of interest.

Herbert Simon introduced the concept of a decision-making process [15–17]. Simon's definition of this process includes four stages:

1. Problem intelligence activity.

2. Problem design activity.

3. Choice activity.

4. Implementation and supervision activity.

In the fourth stage, we may also modify the decision according to feedback, i.e. observation of its effects. The advantage of Simon's approach, however, is that he was the first to pay adequate attention to the role of learning, adaptation, and changing views in the decision-making process.

Herbert Simon formulated a model of satisficing decisions, describable as follows:

a. The decision maker determines aspiration levels for each decision outcome. These aspiration levels are determined adaptively, through a learning process.

b. The choice of decision is not a single act of optimization, but a dynamic process of solution search; in it, the decision maker also learns and may change preferences and aspirations.

c. The process ends when the decision maker finds a decision that achieves an outcome that meets his aspirations (hence the name satisfactory decision) or is in some sense closest to the aspirations.

In this chapter, we discuss the use of vector optimization for decision support.

## 2. Decision-making process model

Most decision-making processes are multi-criteria in nature, that is, they include no single indicator to be optimized so the best decisions are provided. For example, in the design process, an engineer usually tries to find a trade-off between a few indicators, such as reliability and other quality attributes, and on the other hand cost, weight, device volume, etc.

We consider a decision problem defined as a multi-criteria optimization problem with $m$ scalar evaluation functions

$$\max_{x} \{ (f_1(x), \ \dots, \ f_m(x)) : \ x \in X_0 \} \tag{1}$$

where

$f = (f_1, \dots, f_m)$ is a (vector) function that transforms the decision (implementation) space $X = R^n$ into the evaluation space $Y = R^m$; individual coordinates $f_i$ represent scalar evaluation functions; and $I = \{1, 2, \dots m\}$ is a set of evaluation indices.

$X_o \subset X$ is the set of feasible solutions.

$x \in X_o$ is the vector of decision variables.

The function $f$ assigns an evaluation vector $y = f(x)$, which measures the quality of the decision $x$ from the point of view of a fixed set of evaluation functions to each vector of decision variables $x \in X_o f = (f_1, \dots, f_m)$. The formulation of a multi-criteria optimization problem is expressed in decision space. It is a natural representation of the decision problem; its target is the choice of the correct decision. The image of the admissible set $X_o$ for the function $f$ is the set of achievable evaluation vectors $Y_0 = \{y : y = f(x),\ x \in X_0\}$.

The multi-criteria optimization model may be written in an equivalent form in the evaluation space. This leads to a multi-criteria model in the evaluation space:

$$\max_x \{y = (y_1, \ \dots, \ y_m) : \ y_i = f_i(x) \ \forall i, \ \ x \in X_0\} \tag{2}$$

where

$x_o$ is a vector of decision variables.

$y = (y_1, \dots, y_m)$ is a vector of achievable evaluation vectors; the first coordinate is the evaluation function $f_1$ and the last coordinate is the evaluation function $f_m$.

$Y_0 = f(X_0)$ is the set of achievable evaluation vectors.

The set of achievable vectors $Y_0$ is given in an implicit form, i.e., through the set of admissible decisions $X_o$ and the model mapping $f = (f_1, \dots, f_m)$. A simulation of the model $y = f(x)\ for \ \ x \in X_0$ is required to determine $y$.

Each vector $x \in X_o$ corresponds to a vector $y \in Y_0$. The decision maker selects a vector from the set $Y_0$ and chooses for implementation the decision corresponding to that vector from the set $X_0$ [4, 10, 11, 14, 18–20].

The purpose of problem (1) is to help the decision maker choose a decision that is satisfactory to the decision maker.

## 3. Efficient decisions

The solution to a multi-criteria optimization problem is a set of efficient decisions.

Non-dominated solutions (Pareto optimal) are defined by a preference relation that provides an answer to the following question: Which of a given pair of evaluation vectors $y^1, y^2 \in R^m$ is better? This is the following relation:

$$y^1 \succ y^2 \Leftrightarrow y_i^1 \geq y_i^2 \forall i = 1, \dots, m \ \wedge \ \exists j \ y_j^1 > y_j^2 \tag{3}$$

An evaluation vector $\hat{y} \in Y_0$ is called a non-dominated vector if there is no $y \in Y_0$ that the vector $\hat{y}$ which is dominated by the vector $y$ [10, 13, 14, 21–23]. The dominance decision structure in $R^2$ is shown in **Figure 1**.

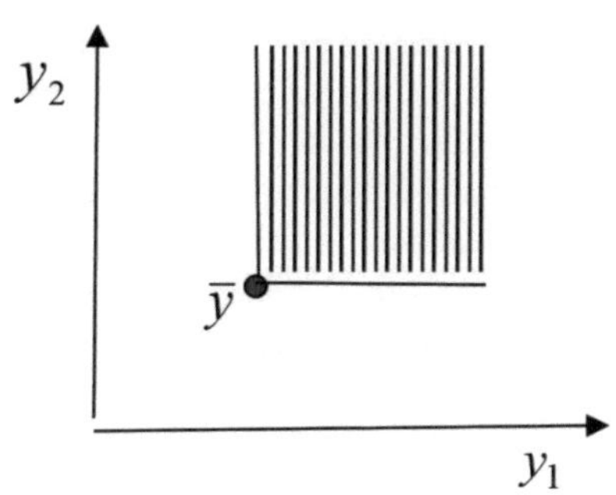


**Figure 1.**
*Dominance structure in $R^2$.*

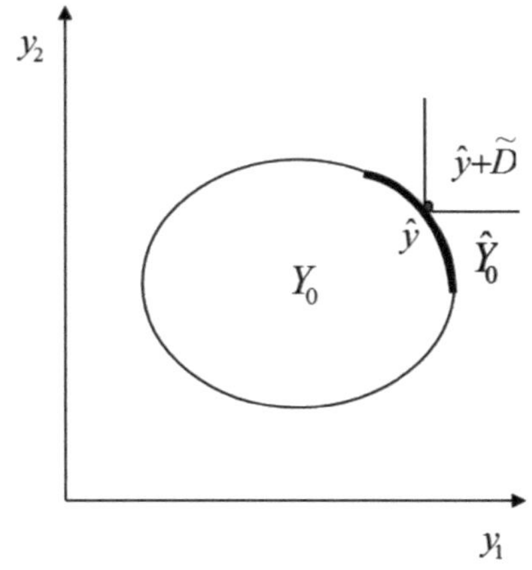


**Figure 2.**
*Non-dominated evaluation vectors* $\hat{Y}_0$ .

The set of non-dominated vectors is defined as follows [10, 14].

$$\hat{Y}_0 = \{\hat{y} \in Y_0 : (\hat{y} + \tilde{D}) \cap Y_0 = \emptyset)\} \quad (4)$$

where

$\tilde{D}$ is a positive cone without a vertex. This positive cone can be as follows: $\tilde{D} = R^m_+$.

The set of non-dominated vectors $\hat{Y}_0$ is shown in **Figure 2**.

The corresponding admissible decisions are defined in the decision space. A decision $\hat{x} \in X_0$ is referred to as an efficient decision (Pareto optimal) if the corresponding evaluation vector $\hat{y} = f(\hat{x})$ is a non-dominated vector.

## 4. Decision support system

The solution to a multi-criteria optimization problem is the entire set of efficient solutions generating a set of all non-dominated evaluation vectors. In the general case, this set may be infinite. In order to solve the decision problem, a single solution must be chosen for implementation. Thus, the set of efficient solutions to a multi-criteria problem may not be regarded as the final solution to the corresponding decision problem.

In multi-criteria decision problems, the decision maker's preference relation is not known a priori, and, therefore, the final choice of the solution may only be made by the decision maker. Due to the size of the set of efficient solutions, even if the entire set of efficient solutions is determined by computational methods, the decision maker may not make the choice of solution without the help of an appropriate interactive information system. Such a system—the decision support system—allows for a controlled review of the set of efficient solutions. Based on the values of certain control parameters given by the decision maker, the system presents different efficient solutions for analysis. Thus, the control parameters determine a certain parameterization of the set of efficient solutions. The parametric analysis of the set of efficient solutions obviates the need to directly determine the entire set of efficient solutions. Instead, the system may each time determine one efficient solution corresponding to the current values of the control parameters. Multi-criteria decision problems are solved by interactive decision support systems using parametric scalarizing of the multi-criteria problem [10, 11, 14, 21]:

$$\max_x \{s(p, f(x)) : \quad x \in X_0\}, \quad p \in P \tag{5}$$

where
$p$ is a vector of control parameters.
$s : P \times Y \to R$ is a scalarizing function.
The scalarizing should satisfy the following conditions:

- efficiency condition—for each vector of control parameters $p \in P$, the optimal solution of the scalar problem was an efficient solution of the original multi-criteria problem;

- condition of completeness of the set of efficient solutions, so that for each non-dominated evaluation vector, there is a set of values of control parameters at which the system determines the efficient solution generating this vector of grades.

The parametric scalarization is then a complete parameterization of the set of efficient solutions to the multi-criteria problem.

The control parameters should represent real quantities that are easily understood by the decision maker and that characterize his preferences. A parametric scalarization that satisfies all of the above postulates makes it possible to implement a decision support system that allows for determination of an efficient solution consistent with the decision maker's preferences.

As the first step of multi-criteria analysis, single-criteria optimization is applied to each evaluation function separately. As a result of single-criteria optimization, a so-called pay-off matrix is created, which allows for estimating the scope of changes of particular evaluation functions on the set of efficient solutions. This matrix also provides some information about the so-called conflict of the evaluation functions. The pay-off matrix is an array containing values of all evaluation functions obtained while solving particular single-criteria problems. The pay-off matrix also generates a utopia vector representing the best values of each evaluation function considered separately, i.e. $y_i^m = \hat{f}_i, i = 1, \dots, m$. The utopia vector is the upper bound of all achievable evaluation vectors, i.e. $y \le y^u$ for each $y \in Y_0$. It is normally unachievable $y^u \notin Y_0$, i.e., there is no admissible solution with such values of evaluation functions. If there exists such an admissible vector $x_0 \in X_0$ so that $f(x_o) = y^u$, then $x_0$ is the optimal solution to the multi-criteria problem in the sense of any preference model. This situation can happen only if there is no conflict between the evaluation functions.

## 5. Reference point method

The reference point method combines the simplicity and openness of controlling the interactive analysis process with strict adherence to the principle of efficiency of the generated solutions and complete parameterization of the set of efficient solutions. The reference point method uses aspiration levels as control parameters and always generates efficient solutions.

The preference model used in the reference point method satisfies the following two postulates:

1. P1—efficient solutions dominate inefficient solutions, i.e., that the decision maker's preferences are consistent with choosing efficient solutions.

2. P2—the decision maker prefers evaluations that achieve all aspiration levels than those that do not achieve one or more aspiration levels.

In this model, it is assumed that when solving a decision problem, the decision maker defines aspiration levels as the desired values of individual evaluations. If the values of the evaluations do not achieve the aspiration levels, the decision maker tries to find a better solution. If the values of some evaluations achieve their respective aspiration levels, the decision maker focuses attention on improving the values of those evaluations that have not achieved their aspiration levels. When all evaluations have achieved their aspiration levels, the decision maker is interested in further improving the evaluations if possible.

The reference point method relies on the minimization of a suitably defined achievement scalarizing function that generates a preference relation satisfying postulates P1 and P2. For that reason, it always determines efficient solutions. It is also required that the achievement scalarizing function ensures the completeness of the parameterization of the set of efficient solutions by aspiration levels. This requirement means that for each achievable evaluation vector $y \in Y_0$, there should be aspiration levels that allow for determining the efficient solution that generates this evaluation vector.

The achievement scalarizing function in the reference point method is as follows [10, 11, 14, 21]:

$$s(y, \bar{y}) = \min_{1 \leq i \leq m} (y_i - \bar{y}_i) + \varepsilon \cdot \sum_{i=1}^{m} (y_i - \bar{y}_i) \tag{6}$$

where

$y = (y_1, y_2, \dots, y_m)$ is an evaluation vector.

$\bar{y} = (\bar{y}_1, \bar{y}_2, \dots, \bar{y}_k)$ is a vector of aspiration levels.

$\varepsilon$—an arbitrarily small regularization parameter.

The maximization of the function $s(y, \bar{y})$ due to $y \in Y_0$ determines the non-dominated evaluation vector $\hat{y}$ and the generating efficient solution $\hat{x}$. The determined efficient solution depends on the values of the aspiration levels $\bar{y}$. The aspiration levels $\bar{y}_i$, $i = 1, \dots, m$ are the parameters that control the interactive analysis process. The parameter $\varepsilon$ is used to introduce a regularization component to guarantee the efficiency of the solution in case of ambiguity of the minimum of the first component of the function $s(y, \bar{y})$.

The optimization problem solved by the reference point method does not introduce significant complications into the structure of the original problem. The process of interactive analysis by the reference point method is consistent with the concept of decision support systems. It implements an open process of searching for a satisficing efficient solution on the basis of current preferences determined by aspiration levels. It is easy for the decision maker to understand the expression of current preferences in terms of aspiration levels.

In the reference point method, the scalarizing function $s(y, \bar{y})$ is called the achievement function. This name is related to the fact that the values of this function are zero for $y = \bar{y}$, positive for $y \in \bar{y} + \tilde{D}$, and negative for $y \notin \bar{y} + \tilde{D}$. Therefore, the maximum values of this function can be used not only to calculate efficient outcomes but also to assess the achievability of a given aspiration point $\bar{y}$:

- If the maximum of the achievement function $s(y, \bar{y})$ relative to $y \in Y_0$ is negative, then the aspiration point $\bar{y}$ is not achievable, while the maximum point $\hat{y}$ of this function is the non-dominated outcome in some sense uniformly closest to the aspiration point $\bar{y}$;

- If the maximum of the achievement function $s(y, \bar{y})$ relative to $y \in Y_0$ is zero, then the aspiration point $\bar{y}$ is an achievable and non-dominated outcome and is (perhaps one of many) the maximum point of this function;

- If the maximum of the achievement function $s(y, \bar{y})$ relative to $y \in Y_0$ is positive, then the aspiration point $\bar{y}$ is achievable, while the maximum point $\hat{y}$ of this function is a non-dominated outcome, in a sense uniformly improved relative to the aspiration point $\bar{y}$.

## 6. Example of application

To illustrate finding a satisficing solution, the following example of a bicriteria problem [24] is presented.

$$
\begin{aligned}
&\max \left\{ \left( f_1(x) = 10 \cdot x_1,\ \ \mathrm{f}_2(x) = x_1 + 5 \cdot x_2 \right) \right\} \\
&\qquad 10 \cdot x_1 \geq 50 \\
&\qquad x_1 \leq 8 \\
&\qquad x_1 + x_2 \leq 14 \\
&\qquad x_1 \geq 0, x_2 \geq 0
\end{aligned}
\tag{7}
$$

The first step of multi-criteria analysis is the single-criteria optimization of each evaluation function is a pay-off matrix containing the values of all functions obtained when solving two single-criteria problems. This matrix allows us to estimate the extent of change of each evaluation function on the possible set, and also provides some information about the conflicting nature of the evaluation function. The objective matrix generates a utopia vector representing the best value of each of the separate criteria (**Table 1**).

The multi-criteria analysis is shown in **Table 2**.

At the beginning of the analysis, the decision maker defines his preference as an aspiration point equal to the utopia vector. The resulting value of the function s is negative. The aspiration point is not achievable. The decision maker's requirements are too high. The obtained solution prefers the first function. To improve the solution for the second function in the next iteration, the decision maker explicitly reduces his requirements for the first function and reduces the requirements for the second function. The value of function s is still negative. The aspiration point is not achieved. The decision maker's requirements are too high. The result is that the solution for the

| Function | Solution | |
|---|---|---|
| | $f_1(x) = y1$ | $f_2(2) = y2$ |
| Function $f_1$ | 140 | 14 |
| Function $f_2$ | 60 | 46 |
| Utopia vector | 140 | 46 |
| *Source: Own calculations.* | | |

**Table 1.**
*Pay-off matrix with utopia vector.*

| Iteration | Solution | | |
|---|---|---|---|
| | $y1$ | | $y2$ |
| 1. Aspiration point $\bar{y}$ | 140 | | 46 |
| Solution $\hat{y}$ | 117.4 | | 23.14 |
| Values | | −22.86 | |
| 2. Aspiration point $\bar{y}$ | 125 | | 42 |
| Solution $\hat{y}$ | 109.28 | | 26.28 |
| Values | | −15.71 | |
| 3. Aspiration point $\bar{y}$ | 115 | | 40 |
| Solution $\hat{y}$ | 103.57 | | 28.57 |
| Values | | −11.43 | |
| 4. Aspiration point $\bar{y}$ | 100 | | 35 |
| Solution $\hat{y}$ | 96.42 | | 31.42 |
| Values | | −3.573 | |
| 5. Aspiration point $\bar{y}$ | 90 | | 35 |
| Solution $\hat{y}$ | 89.28 | | 34.28 |
| Values | | −0.71 | |
| 6. Aspiration point $\bar{y}$ | 85 | | 32 |
| Solution $\hat{y}$ | 87.85 | | 34.85 |
| Values | | 2.85 | |
| 7. Aspiration point $\bar{y}$ | 110 | | 40 |
| Solution $\hat{y}$ | 100 | | 30 |
| Values | | −10.00 | |
| *Source: Own calculations.* | | | |

**Table 2.**
*Interactive analysis of finding a satisfactory solution.*

first function deteriorates and the solution for the second function improves. In the third iteration, the decision maker reduces the requirements for both functions. The value of function s is still negative. The aspiration point is not achieved. The decision maker's requirements are too high. The solution continues to deteriorate for the first function and improves for the second function. In the fourth iteration, the decision maker continues to reduce the requirements for both functions. The value of function s is still negative. The aspiration point is not achieved. The decision maker's requirements are still too high. The solution continues to deteriorate for the first function and improves for the second function. In the fifth iteration, the decision maker continues to reduce the requirements for both functions. The value of function s is still negative. The aspiration point is not achieved. The decision maker's requirements are too high. The solution continues to deteriorate for the first function and improves for the second function. In the sixth iteration, the decision maker continues to reduce the requirements for both functions. The value of function s is now positive. The aspiration point is exceeded. The decision maker's requirements are too small. The solution continues to deteriorate for the first function and improves for the second function. In the seventh iteration, the decision maker increases the requirements for both functions. The value of function s becomes negative. The aspiration point is not achieved. The decision maker's requirements are too high. The solution improves for the first function and deteriorates for the second function. For the seventh iteration, the corresponding decisions are as follows: $\hat{x}^7 = (10,00,\ \ 4,00)$. The analysis shows that the solution depends heavily on the first function and affects the solution more.

The final choice of a particular solution depends on the preferences of the decision maker. The example shows that the method allows the decision maker to explore decision choices during interactive analysis and search for a satisfactory solution.

## 7. Conclusions

This paper presents a decision support system as a multi-criteria optimization problem. The model of the decision problem as a multi-criteria optimization problem allows for generating decision variants and tracking their consequences.

The interactive analysis is based on the reference point method. It allows the decision maker to determine solutions well suited to his preferences. A numerical example shows that the right computational problem can be solved efficiently using standard optimization software.

This type of decision support does not prejudge the final solution but supports and informs the decision maker on the specific decision problem. The final decision is to be made by the decision maker.

## Author details

Andrzej Łodziński
Faculty of Applied Informatics and Mathematics, Warsaw University of Life Sciences, Warsaw, Poland

*Address all correspondence to: and.lodzinski@gmail.com

## References

[1] Alfaris A. Multidisciplinary System Design Optimization: Multiobjective Optimization. MIT OpenCourseWare. Massachusetts Institute of Technology; 2015

[2] Andriole SJ. Handbook of Decision Support Systems. Blue Ridge Summit, PA: TAB Professional and Reference Books; 1989

[3] Aruldoss M, Lakshmi T, Venkatesan V. A Survey on multi criteria decision making methods and its applicationsda. American Journal of Information Systems. 2013;**1**(1): 31-43

[4] Belton SV, Stewart TJ. Multiple Criteria Decision Analysis: an Integrated Approach. Dordrecht, Boston: Kluwer Academic Publishers; 2002

[5] Ehrgott M, Figueira JR, Greco S. Trends in Multiple Criteria Decision Analysis. New York, Dordrecht, Heidelberg, London: Springer; 2010

[6] Fishburn PC. Utility Theory for Decision Making. New York: Wiley; 1970

[7] Goodwin P, Wright G. Analiza decyzji. Warszawa: Wolters Kluwer; 2011

[8] Keeney L, Raiffa H. Decisions with multiple objectives. In: Preferences and Value Tradeoffs. Cambridge University Press; 1993

[9] Luce D, Raiffa H. Gry i decyzje. Warszawa: PWN; 1996

[10] Łodziński A. Interaktywna sposób analizy i podejmowania decyzji wielokryterialnych. Zeszyty Naukowe Politechniki Warszawskiej, 2008. s. 301-309

[11] Ogryczak W. Wielokryterialna optymalizacja liniowa i dyskretna modele preferencji i zastosowania do wspomagania decyzji Uniwersytet Warszawski Instytut Informatyk Warszawa. 1997

[12] Roy B. Multicriteria Methodology for Decision Aiding. Dordrecht: Kluwer Academic Publishers; 1996

[13] Trzaskalik T. Wielokryterialne wspomaganie decyzji. Metody i zastosowania. Warszawa: PWE; 2014

[14] Wierzbicki AP. Teoria i praktyka wspomagania decyzji Copyright by Wydawnictwa Uniwersytetu Warszawskiego, Warszawa, 2018

[15] Simon HA. Models of Man – Social and Rational. New York: J. Wiley; 1957

[16] Simon HA. Administrative Behavior. New York: The Macmillan Company; 1958

[17] Steuer RE. Multiple Criteria Optimization: Theory, Computation and Application. New York: J. Wiley; 1986

[18] Łodziński A. System wspomagania decydenta w podejmowaniu decyzji zadawalających. Zeszyty naukowe AGH, Zagadnienia techniczno – ekonomiczne, Uczelniane Wydawnictwo Naukowo – Dydaktyczne AGH, Kraków, 2007. pp. 159–165

[19] Rezaei J. Best-worst multi-criteria decision-making method. Omega the International Journal of Management Science. 2015;**53**:49-57

[20] Zimmermann H-J, Gutsche L. Multi-Criteria Analyse: Einfuhrung in die Theorie der Entscheidungen bei

Mehrfachzielsetzungen. Berlin: Springer-Verlag; 1991

[21] Lewandowski A, Wierzbicki A, editors. Aspiration based decision support systems. European Journal of Operational Research. Berlin-Heidelberg: Springer-Verlag; 1989

[22] Waters D. Quantitative Methods for Business. Upper Sadle River: Prentice Hall; 2011

[23] Wierzbicki AP. A mathematical basis for satisficing decision making. Mathematical Modelling. 1982;**3**:391-405

[24] Shi Y, Yu PL, Scupin A. Goal setting and compromise solutions. In: Karpak B, Zionts S, editors. Multiple Criteria Decision Making and Risk Analysis Using Microcomputers. Vol. Series, Vol. F56. Berlin Heidelberg New York London Paris Tokyo Hong Kong: Springer-Verlag; 1987. pp. 165-205 Published in cooperation with NATO Scientific Affairs Division

Section 4

# A New Perspective on Cognitive Decision-Making Process

Chapter 7

# Perspective Chapter: A Perspective on Cognitive Decision-Making in Dynamic Systems – Are Decision Failures Indicators for a Mutation toward Processing New Concepts?

*Bernard Cadet and Isabel Cuadrado Gordillo*


## Abstract

In numerous scientific disciplines, the decision-making process aims at choosing the most appropriate action to reach a defined objective is a central issue. Scientific literature demonstrates that a wide range of often prescriptive models is available to deal with this sequence. However, one category of situations, involving the intervention of complex, dynamic, and changeable systems (a forest fire for example) generate imprecisions, difficulties, or even incorrect decisions. This largely prospective chapter aims to study these situations from a cognitive point of view to reveal certain recurrent properties of their operation. These indicators may represent milestones for the construction of a new epistemology that would refer to the globality and the dynamism rather than to isolated and analytical entities.


**Keywords:** decision-making in systems, failures as positive indicators, epistemology and cognition, complex systems and cognitive psychology, decision-making evolution

## 1. Introduction

People frequently say that the objective of scientific research is to pursue knowledge to take appropriate action over the world. Adhering to this principle involves special epistemological procedures both as regards the information selection and how it is organized. This document will discuss the diagnosis and decision-making activities, in complex systems. The six sections of this chapter aim to introduce a few fundamental properties to be taken into consideration in the action choices. Section 1 emphasizes that the choice of action is a mental (cognitive) construction to be performed in each occurrence. Section 2 presents the paradigm as a tool for processing information. Section 3 examines the structure of paradigms that aim *objectivity*. In Section 4, examined paradigms aim to ensure that the action is adequate and *appropriate* to achieve the desired result. Section 5 recommends a change in format to study societal or group decision makings. Section 6 analyses decision-making as a dynamic process made from interactions between sub-systems. Section 7 evaluates the possible consequences of the notions of complexity and dynamism on the subsequent evolution of psychology.

Various epistemological processes will be analyzed, not only as regards their intrinsic content (the case being processed), but also with respect to their contribution to the general evolution of the discipline toward new conceptions and innovative epistemological repositioning using systems rather than variables.

## 2. Cognitive decision-making from a constructivist perspective

### 2.1 Salient characteristics

Reduced to its most basic characteristics, decision-making process consists in choosing one specific action amongst those available, than in performing it effectively to obtain the desired effect. The chosen action must be relevant since it meets a requirement. Its implementation must obviously modify the situation in the desired direction. To achieve this effect, a diagnosis must first be made. It consists of a cognitive construction that includes the information selected and processed by the decision-maker[1] as in medical diagnosis.

### 2.2 A constructed choice and its consequences

How is the choice made? The decision maker's cognitive activity expresses this preference. It refers to the constructivism theory developed at an early stage by Jean Piaget [1, 2]. This pioneering author demonstrated that cognition is far from being an innate characteristic or a predetermined choice of action.

A fundamental epistemological principle must already be laid down the appropriate action choice is not only established on the general properties of certain information. It must also incorporate situational and temporal particularisms. Such a perspective is well illustrated in decisions regarding diagnosis and decision-making issues (in medicine or engineering sciences for instance). The general properties of an illness are given by the nosography, but the particularities result from an individual examination carried out by a clinician.

Nowadays, constructivism has gone far beyond its initial target (the study of reasoning modes in infancy) to be implemented, thanks to technological progress, in social contexts [3]. This current of studies has its distant roots in the work of Vygotsky (1896–1936) in terms of the decision that will be analyzed. The introduction of reference to social groups allows us to study social decisions and social choices. Referring to groups permits to include collective problem-solving and studying group decision-making and its effects on population or social groups, such as acceptability of laws.

### 2.3 Information: Collecting and formatting in a system

This chapter studies situations in which information is organized in systems. Following a seminal work [4] and for psychologists "A system can be defined as a set of elements that interact with each other." Decision-making is studied in

[1] To avoid the complexity of inclusive writing, the masculine gender will be used herein. It takes a generic meaning to designate the human being. Its use is therefore not intended to be discriminatory toward anyone.

self-organized systems where all information is organized into interactive systems that, at first glance, seem complex and need a cognitive treatment to be read.

## 3. The paradigm as a tool

### 3.1 Definition

The paradigm is defined as being a "dominant theoretical concept taking place during a certain period in a given scientific community, which lays down the possible types of explanation and the types of fact to be discovered in a given science." Note the extreme caution and relativism demonstrated by the authors of this definition[2].

### 3.2 Specificity

Decision-making is not limited to accumulating information. To be useful, the collected set needs to be organized and structured in order to make it easier to choose appropriate action. Human cognitive abilities are indeed limited not only in working memory but also in various other cognitive tasks (limited perceptual empan (items of information not perceived); illusory correlations, misinterpretations, conservatism, etc. [5]. The operations prescribed by the paradigm can be considered as guarantees against discrepancies in collecting a set of compatible information. Cognitive decision-making (CDM) tasks as a whole need to be constructed taking into account the characteristics of each occurrence. We may, therefore, already think that initially applying general treatment strategies does not appear to be a suitable choice.

### 3.3 Internal compatibility

Widely used in human and social sciences, the paradigm ensures the consistency and compatibility of the various steps involved in a research approach. This means that the chosen reference theory, the methodology used, the nature of the collected data, and their processing modalities need to be made compatible.

The criterion that such compatibility has been achieved is empirical. It translates experienced people (experts for instance), into fluidity of the linking of the different processing operations when constructing the choice of action.

Choosing an appropriate paradigm is one of the most important cognitive operations to perform to set up the epistemological framework necessary for CDM.

### 3.4 Epistemological indicator

Paradigms' functions are not, however, limited to these aspects, which can be qualified as internal. In addition to these properties, it is useful to add a new function of any paradigm: its operating value. A paradigm is also a tool set up to produce convergence in information and ultimately achieve a single final action value, which is better than any other.

---

[2] *Bibliographic note: CNRLT Ortolang. Centre National de Ressources Textuelles et Lexicales (National Centre for Textual and Lexical Resources). Definition of paradigm [Translated from the French by the authors].

Kuhn [6] gives it a function indicating whether a paradigm is adapted to the problems it studies. When a given paradigm repeatedly fails to deal with concrete situations, a shift to another one is essential. Referring to the title of the book by Kuhn, we are talking about a "scientific revolution," which marks the need to build and use a new paradigm that performs better.

Currently, psychologists mainly use two kinds of paradigms (P1 and P2) to construct CDM. Paradigms of type 1 (a.k.a. P1 type) search for an *objective* choice of action; those of type 2 (a.k.a. P2 type) are looking for an *appropriate* choice.

## 4. Paradigms of P1 type used in CDM

### 4.1 Paradigms that search for "objectivity" (type 1)

The implemented action, with a high degree of probability, makes the expected changes to the situation or obtain the expected advantages. This implicit but prevailing condition has led researchers in human sciences to valorize the quest for objectivation. They adopted a paradigm that, since the mid-nineteenth century, has largely demonstrated its efficiency: the objective experimental paradigm (OEP).

### 4.2 The objective experimental paradigm (OEP)

Although attempts were made previously, particularly in physics and chemistry, it appeared for the first time in the book by Claude Bernard [6] dedicated to medicine. Since then, the approach has witnessed numerous "aggiornamento" and is now considered to be an organized series of well-defined operations [7]. In view of its undeniable successes, in a wide range of disciplines, extending from the formalized sciences to the human and social sciences, at the present time, those adhering to the qualities of objectivity and replicability consider that the OEP and the experimental approach underlie numerous research strategies.

The purpose of this chapter is not to provide an exhaustive analysis of this approach, which specialized reviews do very well [8, 9]. We will simply make comments on two characteristics of this method; a *place* (the laboratory) and a *strategy* (in processing information).

### 4.3 The laboratory: A privileged location

So that it can be applied, the experimental method must be implemented in a special location, protected from external influences considered to be disturbing: the laboratory. Used systematically in the material and life sciences, it was used for the first time in psychology by Wundt in 1879. Wundt wanted to make psychology a science by aligning the research studies with the procedures used in physiology.

While the laboratory led to the definition of the psychophysical laws concerning the relations between perception and sensation, it only became widely used following Pavlov's studies on conditioning and Watson's behaviorist theory, resulting in the emergence of experimental psychology. More recently, cognitive psychology uses experimental approaches in the study of brain activity in relation to the fundamental conduct of the human being.

The main feature of the laboratory is that it is carefully isolated from the outside world which is, in fact, *a priori* considered as a source of disturbance (interference variables). We remember the "towers of silence" built by Pavlov to study conditioning. The laboratory provides controlled conditions under which reasoned operations can be conducted on properties considered, by assumption, as being essential.

### 4.4 An adapted strategy

The laboratory also implies the use of a quite specific epistemology whose function is to "eliminate" from the system the momentary or incident characteristics which exist in concrete situations. The purpose of the epistemological section is to reveal fundamental information, which is always present under all circumstances. To achieve this, the situation studied will be reduced to a set of relations considered by the researcher as being fundamental while excluding, whenever possible, all the others. This cognitive operation is the first step of *scientific reductionism,* which will be accompanied by a second epistemological section.

A *deconstruction-reconstruction* strategy is then implemented and applied to what could be considered as being a cognitive model of the actual situation. Variables are isolated, processed, removed, added, correlated, etc. using procedures intended to reveal their effects and their relations. By manipulating or acting, using an ad hoc device built in the laboratory, any variations observed in the entity studied can finally be recorded.

### 4.5 The cognitive consequences

As implied by the etymology of the word, epistemology is a branch of philosophy concerned with knowledge. This knowledge stems from the choices of researchers at the two levels of cognition: first collection and then organization of the information collected. The resulting knowledge will depend on the initial stamp of the choices made at these two cognitive levels. These two operations will foster what can be considered a simplified mental reconstruction of the situation rather that the situation itself, which will then only appear in the background.

At this stage, the search for simplification still prevails, in a different form, by explicitly seeking *parsimony* [10] of the explanation (often called Occam's razor). Let us take the example of a researcher who would have two distinct mental constructions explaining the same conduct with equal efficiency; application of the parsimony criterion would lead us to choose the simplest form. However, this type of simplifying approach to knowledge has its downsides, which will appear—which is not at all paradoxical—with the progress of knowledge.

## 5. Paradigms of P2 type used in CDM

### 5.1 Paradigm looking for an appropriate choice

One of the main criticisms of the objective experimental paradigm is its highly analytical nature. The initial breakdown into elementary units (or considered as such) does not guarantee that the conduct studied will not lose some of its fundamental aspects, which is all the more likely if the entity studied is complex, like all human conducts.

One of the strategies selected to dismiss this risk simply consists of referring to totality as a source of information. In this paradigm, the very idea of looking for variables is abandoned, and the situation will be considered as an entity whose global configuration must be respected.

This choice turns out to be quite the opposite of the analytical approaches conducted in the laboratory, which consider globality as being an obstacle to knowledge. The question is nevertheless worthy of being discussed at the cost of an epistemological revolution, can we consider that the concept of globality is a provider of information?

### 5.2 The processing of globality

Regarding this aspect, psychology may claim a concept developed in the middle of the twentieth century, first in Germany, then in the United States, by psychologist Kurt Lewin. Considered one of the founders of Gestalt Psychology, this author recommends considering conducts (and choices) as global entities which cannot be reduced to the sum of their parts. Globality has its own specific properties: it, therefore, provides information that will be lost if any analytical reduction attempt is made.

Gestalt psychologists are known by the public for having provided examples that involve visual perception applied to reversible figures, demonstrating that the "background" and the "shape" can be alternated. The same graphical representation results in the successive perception of *two* quite different objects or scenes. Far from being merely entertaining, these situations, widely published in magazines, identify two epistemological properties. Firstly, the figure "stands out" from the background *dynamically*, suggesting the underlying presence of active forces. Secondly, the functional alternations imply (semi-) global entities, that is, the figure and the background, but which only have temporary perceptive status. Apart from the dynamism, this type of phenomenon reveals the relativism of visual perception too often considered objective and, finally, may question the validity of the visual testimony.

### 5.3 The contributions of the gestalt paradigm

The psychological Gestalt concepts have introduced new strategies in the construction of decision-making conduct. The two main references concerning the purpose of this conceptual current are the notions of *force* and of *field*, both used in physics. The decision-making process involves several forces and the action selected is in some respects, the result of a system.

Inventor of action research, promoter of group techniques, and author of a fundamental book, Lewin [11] introduced numerous innovations in psychological research. He emphasizes the importance of the field (environment) and of the time when processing takes place, and alongside this time perspective, he introduces the notion of forces as a determining factor in the choice of action (these properties being adapted to decision-making). Applying the fundamental Gestalt principle, these field characteristics, even when they are evaluated by the same decision-maker, do not necessarily have either the same value or a fixed nature since the time, the environment and objectives of the planned action may vary.

Lewin's premature death and the absence at the time of a methodological framework adapted to the treatment of these notions temporarily limited the scope of these concepts, some of which were only to be confirmed several decades later. We will remember from this trend that the laws stated concern the organization and the properties of the object studied in its entirety and not, as in the OEP, the method used to do so.

On a different subject, the studies conducted by Edwards [12, 13] represent a determining milestone in the "psychologization" of decision-making. By involving the decision-maker from the start of the processing method as a stakeholder in the construction of the situation (and no longer as an arbitrator who chooses the action at the end of the processing), these contributions will allow new types of processing.

### 5.4 The notion of facet

As described in the previous paragraph, decision-making consists in identifying an underlying entity (a risk, a critical situation, a state, a disease, etc.) using signs that it produces, which can be observed or even measured in the outside world. The entity is considered in its entirety as being the common origin of the observed or measured signs also called facets, although they are nevertheless varied. This diversity deserves to be considered positively since the variety and diversity of the signs are desirable in order to decrease the initial uncertainty more rapidly.

However, even more than their number, the determining factor is consistency, a cognitive quality that reflects whether the signs are compatible with each other during the various processing operations. The inference approach regarding the nature of the entity concerned requires diversity rather than repetitiveness. The aim is therefore to collect different but consistent signs. For instance, it is possible to identify the composer of a piece of classical music from facets characterizing his style.

### 5.5 Facets and informational contents

Every facet is an observable expression issued by an underlying entity. It provides information from the outset regarding the source which produced it, so that action can be taken on this source.

Spontaneously, the facet has two epistemological qualities. Firstly, it is multi-determined due to the large number of conditions accounting for its appearance and resulting from interactions. Secondly, each facet has a quality label: it naturally shows the result of interactive effects without having to conceive them in an abstract manner before testing them. The facets result in fact neither from an experimental plan nor from a hybrid created according to previously selected procedures. The facet is determined from *tangible* influences, not from abstract suppositions.

## 6. A change of format for decision-making situations

### 6.1 A positioning in a natural, open space

By abandoning the laboratory and its associated methods, it will be possible to study new types of situations and direct the interest of researchers toward the processing of decision-making or prediction situations treated *in situ*. In view of the need for knowledge related to social evolution, psychologists have had to deal with a completely different type of decision-making, in which the effects are not expected but have already been produced. As a result, situations in natural environment (i.e., outside the laboratory) must be taken into account; these situations include numerous variables which are often difficult to identify and which generally include interactions at various levels.

Some concrete examples of this change of structure and of the decision-making difficulties it generates are deeply engraved in social memory. The collective memory was marked by the forest fires in California (summer of 2018) and the bushfires in Australia spreading rapidly from December 2019[3] and which would only be brought under control in March 2020 despite the considerable firefighting means implemented.

### 6.2 Social decisions

These situations receiving wide media coverage include (in particular) forest fires and pollution.

Decision-making difficulties are also encountered in similar forms in the management of marine pollution due to oil spills from tankers. There are numerous examples. We will only mention three of the most well-known. The Amoco Cadiz (1978) [14] caused major pollution after sinking off the Brittany coast (France); in a similar event, the Exxon Valdez (1989) seriously polluted the Alaska coastline and the sinking of the Prestige (2002) led to an ecological disaster with a major tourist and economic impact to the northwest coastline of the Iberian Peninsula.

Other situations of identical architecture, such as management of a pandemic or of global warming place, the decision-makers in situations in which they are faced with cognitive obstacles. Unlike the previous paradigm, the decision-makers are not responsible for creating the situations, they simply observe that they exist and that they have their own dynamics.

### 6.3 Interpersonal decisions

On another level, which confirms that it really is the architecture of the situation and not only the number of persons concerned, which must be considered, we find two recurrent societal issues. There is in fact a need to make decisions rapidly to deal with situations involving clearly identified individuals or social groups. In this respect, two types of situations are characteristic: firstly, family violence and abuse by adults on children, and secondly, school or group harassment by peers.

The studies conducted on bullying Refs. [15, 16] demonstrated that while the conduct of the persons involved, aggressors and victims, depended on personal psychological characteristics, those of the field (cyberspace) played a determining role in the expression of their intensity, their permanency or their termination.

Whether social, within the meaning of the group, or social, within the meaning of the presence of another person, these situations require a different epistemological position.

## 7. An epistemological shift: intermediate and complex systems

### 7.1 A necessary intermediate formation

At the time of Gestalt, since no suitable epistemological framework was available, the Gestalt concepts were easy to observe (descriptive validity) but difficult to use in practice (predictive validity). One of the missing links, not mentioned by these authors, is that of sub-systems. The authors concerned, focusing mainly on demonstrating the globality of the conduct studied, took little interest in its determinants.

[3] Which corresponds to austral summer.

They simply stated descriptive "laws," emphasizing the characteristics of the entities to be processed.

At a very early stage, two psychologists [17] demonstrated, from a completely different perspective, the existence of intermediate structures or formations, of different types, between the information present at the input of the processing system and the behaviors or conclusions observed at the output.

These authors point out the intervention of the intermediate systems that operate between these two poles and play a structuring role in processing the message. A fundamental transformation concerns the sensorial inputs, which, from the outset, are assigned a meaning which gives them a cognitive status. For visual perception, for instance, the metaphor of the camera and of the objectivity of the perception proves to be more a post hoc reconstruction than a reality.

### 7.2 An epistemological breakthrough

Since then, the progress made by research in other disciplines (in particular, meteorology, nonlinear bonds, astrophysics, and thermodynamics) encourages researchers to postulate that these intermediate systems (which are in actual fact sub-systems) determine the characteristics and evolution of the entire system.

The discovery of the underlying dynamics had such an impact that it shook the foundations of epistemological concepts, which had been considered as reliable guides for several decades. It is, particularly, well expressed in the famous assertion of the flap of a butterfly's wing by Lorenz in 1972 which, after a period of cognitive disarray clearly reflected by the term "theory of chaos," led to a new way of building science [18]. The scientific study of these new situations is no longer compatible with the intangible framework of earlier epistemological conceptions (Descartes, Newton, Laplace). In contrast, the notions of system, sub-system, ambient environment, and internal forces will form novel tools, adapted to the study of the underlying dynamics.

### 7.3 Epistemological theorization

In 1968, as said before [4], a book was published that emphasized the usefulness of the notion of system as an epistemological framework relevant to numerous scientific disciplines (including psychology). A more recent contribution [19] provides a recent update on how the theory of complex systems is (or could be) used in the social sciences.

The initial contribution brings arguments to use a unifying theory of complex systems. Beyond the specificities of each discipline, a common background looms[4].

### 7.4 Some important methodological features

Very briefly outlined, the selected situations share well-known structural and functional properties.

- A system is a global structure (forming a whole) composed of elements (basic units) interacting in various ways.

- The relations between globality and elements cannot be reduced to the sum of the parts.

[4] Note the singular used in the title of the first edition of the book: *General System Theory*.

- These interactions are generally nonlinear and may vary over time, which automatically prevents the use of arithmetic proportionality for the inference.

- The system is dynamic. It evolves "spontaneously" (i.e., on its own resources) depending on the conditions it encounters in its environment).

- When human operators want to control or direct the subsequent evolution of the system using "governance" process (i.e., put out a forest fire or reduce a pandemic), the system may "resist." From a behavioral point of view, this results in a failure of the methods implemented by the operators to control the situation.

The temporal dimension, unlike the previous paradigms, the paradigm of complex systems places significant emphasis on the temporal dimension. The initial states of the system, which are essential to determine their subsequent evolution, must be known. It is also useful to specify the mental or cognitive patterns of the decision-makers and, if possible, to know the type of paradigm to which they are initially referring (which is generally not taken into account).

## 8. The contributions of the paradigm of dynamic systems on the evolution of psychology

### 8.1 Paradigm of dynamic systems

The psychological decision-making processes do not only provide substantive indications (i.e., specific to each case). By adopting a transverse and, therefore, chronological perspective, the evolution of psychology can be characterized using internal factors that are responsible for its mutations or progress. A first observation shows that evolution is not linear. It is not based on continuous capitalization of knowledge but improves, as pointed out by Kuhn, in successive steps, from one paradigm to the next that has a higher explanatory potential. A second comment concerns the homogeneity versus heterogeneity factor. Homogeneity is a paradigm *infra* quality since each decision conduct, irrespective of its specificities will be built using the concepts and methods present in the paradigm, which, thus proves to be an operational reserve. Heterogeneity is a paradigm *supra* quality. It indicates paradigm changes.

### 8.2 The decisionmaker's cognitive activities

The succession of decision-making paradigms is indicative of a double concern experienced by researchers. Firstly, avoid any form of extreme reductionism or simplification of the problems. Secondly, the need to build a satisfactory and efficient mental representation of the dynamics of phenomena capable of extending beyond the perceived complexity. The decision-maker selects the information according to the properties of the paradigms.

The OEP does not avoid the first obstacle but provides, due to its simplicity, a topographic cognitive map, which, although incomplete, is easy to use. The paradigm of the dynamic systems does not avoid the second obstacle when it attempts to evaluate functional quantities, in other words momentary landmarks of the operation and not of the structure.

The decision maker's cognitive status and the type of operations to be performed will be different as soon as the initial choice of paradigm has been made. Each researcher initially opts for a school of thought whose opinions or ideas he shares. The choice of processing methods primarily depends on the decision-maker's personal options.

### 8.3 Overall lessons learned

How can we summarize the quasi-temporal succession of the paradigms described in this chapter?

- The first is organized so as to obtain a quality that is fundamental to the action: its objective nature. To achieve this, the simplification condition is applied.

- The second, probably chosen as a reaction against the outrageous applications that distort the subject of the studies, decides to process it in its natural position and its globality.

- The third is defined by focusing on the notions of organization into systems (at several levels) of dynamism and of forces and insertion in an open, active, and changing context.

### 8.4 Does negative become positive?

In many respects, the paradigm of complex systems results in making radical changes to the status of some characteristics of the information. A Copernic revolution occurs what was previously considered negatively and, in this respect, controlled and eliminated from OEP-type processing, becomes, in the perspective of dynamic systems, a source of information.

As we have seen, the laboratory used to isolate the situation studied from the outside world becomes a distorting mirror. Similarly, the decision-maker is assumed to be in a position of relative cognitive neutrality. His opinion is not finalized, leading him to examine numerous partial assumptions. In contrast, in situations of recognized complexity, the decision-maker uses a cognitive block from the outset. This knowledge tool consists of the information present in the situation and analysis registers controlled by the decision-maker. The individual and the situation must therefore be considered as a whole, without splitting them.

This type of recommendation involves major epistemological extensions since the specificity of each cognitive block takes priority over its general nature. Based on this observation, we see that, for numerous situations displaying differences initially considered as minor, it is unrealistic or even deceitful to apply exactly the same processing method on the mere grounds of a previous success. Each situation/decision-maker block has its own specificities and we know that, in complex systems, minor differences at the start of the processing may generate fundamental differences in the conclusions. As a result, the decision-making activity in the systems must also look for, in addition to the general aspects, the specificities and variabilities, since they are sources of information.

## 9. Conclusion

Three key steps can be identified in this chapter. Each one represents a polarization of the research approach toward an organized objective in a paradigm. The first group of researchers [5, 8–10], naturally focused on objectivity, considering the scientific context of their time. Without abandoning the search for this quality, their successors [4, 11, 18, 19] realized that the very high domination of method over subject led to conclusions, which, although correct, were difficult to transpose to the reality of the situations.

The adoption of new investigation approaches is characterized by three options: process the globality, process the conducts in natural environment, consider the forces and the dynamisms of systems (and sub-systems where applicable). Applied to decision-making processes in special situations, these new approaches also have a very strong impact on the overall evolution of psychology and on its mutations toward new boundaries.

## Author details

Bernard Cadet[1*] and Isabel Cuadrado Gordillo[2]

1 University of Normandy, Caen, France

2 University of Estremadura, Badajoz, Spain

*Address all correspondence to: bernard.cadet50@gmail.com

## References

[1] Tobin K, Tipping D. Constructivism as a referent for teaching and learning. In: Tobin K, editor. The Practice of Constructivism in Science Education. Hillsdale NJ: Lawrence Erlbaum; 1993. pp. 3-21

[2] Chalon Blanc A. Constructivisme. Intelligence. L'avenir d'une théorie. Villeneuve d'Ascq: Presses Universitaires du Septentrion; 2011

[3] Jackson P. Technologies and the Enterprise. Web 2.0 Knowledge. Smarter, Lighter and Cheaper. Witney: Chandos Publishing; 2010

[4] von Bertalanffy L. General Systems Theory. Foundations, Development, Applications. New York: George Brazillier; 1968

[5] Hogarth RM. Decision-Making, Judgment and Choice. New York: Wiley; 1987

[6] Bernard C. Introduction à l'étude de la médecine expérimentale. Paris: Baillière; 1865 [In French]

[7] Kuhn TS. The Structure of Scientific Revolutions. Chicago: Chicago University Press; 1970

[8] Healy AF. Handbook of Experimental Psychology. New York: Wiley; 2008

[9] Davis, S.F.0. Handbook of Research Methods in Experimental Psychology. Oxford (UK): Blackwell Publishing; 2003

[10] Sober E. Parsimony arguments in science and philosophy-a test case for naturalism. Proceedings and addresses of the. American Philosophical Association. 2009;**83**(2):117-156 JSTOR Retrieved on June 8, 2021

[11] Lewin K. Principles of Topological Psychology. New York: Mac Graw Hill; 1936

[12] Edwards W. Behavioral decision-making. Annual Review of Psychology. 1961;**12**:473-488

[13] Edwards W. Conservatism in human information processing. In: Kleinmuntz B, editor. Formal Representation of Human Judgment. New York: Wiley; 1968. pp. 17-52

[14] Chelminski R. Superwreck. Amoco Cadiz. The Shipwreck That Had to Happen. New York: William Morrow; 1987

[15] Cuadrado-Gordillo I, Fernandez-Antelo I. Cyberspace as a generator of changes in the aggressive-victim role. Computers in Human Behavior. 2014;**30**:225-233

[16] Cuadrado-Gordillo I, Fernandez-Antelo I. Adolescents' perception of the characterizing dimensions of cyberbullying: Differentiation between bullies' and victims' perceptions. Computers in Human Behavior. 2016;**55**:653-663

[17] MacCorquodale K, Meehl P. On a distinction between hypothetical constructs and intervening variables. Psychological Review. 1948;**55**:95-107

[18] Dizikes P. When the butterfly effect took flight. MIT Review. 22 Feb 2011. Retrieved MIT Review: https://www.technologyreview.com/2011/02/22/196987/when-the-butterfly-effect-took-flight/

[19] Byrne D, Callaghan G. Complexity Theory and the Social Sciences. London: CRC Press; 2013